THE DIARY OF VASLAV NIJINSKY

Nijinsky in SCHEHEREZADE

The Diary of
Vaslav Nijinsky

Edited by
ROMOLA NIJINSKY

UNIVERSITY OF CALIFORNIA PRESS

BERKELEY AND LOS ANGELES

University of California Press

Berkeley and Los Angeles, California

All Rights Reserved

Copyright, 1936, by Simon and Schuster, Inc.

ISBN: 0-520-00945-2

Library of Congress Catalog Card Number: 68-124626

First Paper-bound Edition

Third Printing, 1973

Manufactured in the United States of America

ACKNOWLEDGMENT

I wish to thank Lady Ottoline and Mr. Philip Morrell for their indefatigable efforts on behalf of the NIJINSKY FOUNDATION, *Mr. Edward Warburg of New York for his generous contribution, Mr. John R. Sutro and Captain Bruce Ottley of London for their interest in the welfare of Nijinsky, and finally Mr. Alfred Robert Shaw for his ever-present kindness, help, and friendship.*

I also want to express my thanks to Miss Jennifer Mattingly for assisting me in the translation of the Diary.

CONTENTS

LIST OF ILLUSTRATIONS

The portraits of Nijinsky are from the private collection of Mr. Roger Pryor Dodge.

PREFACE

THIS Diary *is Nijinsky's message to mankind. His expressed desire to have it published during his lifetime was fulfilled when it first appeared in 1936.*

It is a rare human document; very few of the great artists of the world have so frankly given us in writing their ideas about religion, art, love, and life as my husband does in these "confessions." The fact that he wrote his Diary *at a time when he was experiencing extreme mental agony and that he was yet able to communicate so lucidly his feelings, gives it a profoundly moving quality and makes it truly unique.*

The Diary *was written during 1918-19 in St. Moritz where we had retired to await the end of the war.*

Isolated from the world, from all possibilities of exercising his art, my husband tried to reach the masses through other artistic mediums. He took up drawing and music, created choreographies, and finally wrote his Diary.

In editing this Diary *I have kept to the original text and used, as far as possible, the same expressions as Nijinsky himself. Some of the incidents related by my husband in his "confessions" have already been described in my first book. In their present form they show his interpretation of these incidents.*

He wrote feverishly for hours and hours, day and night. I tried to stop him, as I feared he would be exhausted. I felt that slowly, mercilessly, he was being drawn away from his art, his life, and me by an uncanny, invisible power. I fought, desperately terrified, against this ghastly force. I could not explain what had happened, for I only sensed

[xi]

the change. My husband was kind, generous, as loving as ever, yet, in spite of this, a different person. I tried to understand him but he evaded my questions. Then I wanted to read the Diary to find the solution, but he would not permit it. For months he kept his Diary locked up; then he promised to give it to me. When the dreadful calamity had befallen us, and we realized that Nijinsky was ill, the Diary and everything else were utterly forgotten, and the great struggle began to save him from insanity.

The Diary was accidentally rediscovered in June, 1934; my first book on Nijinsky was published at the time. An exhibition was organized, and I was asked to lend my own collection. In searching for some costumes, I remembered that a few trunks had been left in storage in 1919. In those, among other objects, four school exercise books were found. Thought to belong to our daughter, they were put aside. Months later I looked at them and noticed they were written in my husband's own writing. The contents were translated from the Russian and Nijinsky's memoirs revealed.

With the exception of Noverre, no dancer ever expressed himself so openly. Nijinsky was known to the world as a great dancer—the Dieu de la danse—but he was more: he was a humanitarian, a seeker of truth, whose only aim was to help, to share, to love.

He devoted all his life, his soul, his genius, to the service of humanity, with the intention of ennobling and uplifting his audience, to bring art, beauty, and joy to the world. His aim was not to entertain or to reap success and glory for himself, but to transmit a divine message through his own medium—the dance. He could not escape, with his incorporeal, sensitive nature, the fate of all great humanitarians—to be sacrificed.

I am convinced that had he found more understanding, more gentleness, among those who surrounded him, including myself, he would have been spared the terrible *mental anguish which eventually forced him to withdraw from the world of reality into a world of his own.*

In early youth he learned to know the hardships of life. He witnessed his mother's unhappiness and poverty; he patiently supported, during the eight years spent in the Imperial School, the petty jealousies of his classmates, later the oppression to which, as a young dancer, he was exposed. His fellow artists, the members of the Russian Ballet, were often antagonistic, and he did not even find understanding among those he helped to attain fame and success, through his extraordinary talent, visionary creations, and unceasing efforts. They tried to take away all his merits, but how could they understand Nijinsky, his pure heart, his humility, his childlike faith in Art, Beauty, and God? These were beyond their comprehension.

In all its history, only one other genius of the dance was attacked as much as Nijinsky: Noverre, who also was persecuted, accused of not having composed his own immortal ballets, and misunderstood utterly by his colleagues. Nijinsky and Noverre, the two great reformers of the art of dancing. . . . Nijinsky was aware of all this enmity, and still he did not want to give up his belief in human kindness. The blow came when his faith in friendship was shattered, and he went on quietly, forgivingly, until the great massacre, World War I, and his inability to help humanity broke his heart. Then he "retired in himself so far that he he could no longer understand the people."

In the years following the onslaught of my husband's illness, it was our fate to experience much cruelty and unhappiness. Indeed, we often lived like wandering gypsies, especially during the years of World War II, never knowing from one day to the next if we would have a roof over our heads when night fell.

Preface

When my husband first became ill I dreaded having to confine him to an asylum, even though the psychiatrists advised me to do so. I decided instead to keep him at our home in St. Moritz where I could care for him and where I thought he would be happier with his freedom and family life. But later I realized the doctors were right, and Nijinsky was taken to a sanatorium, to which I accompanied him. I tried to secure for him the best help possible, and, after consulting the most prominent specialists, including Freud and Jung, we spent several months in Vienna where Nijinsky was cared for in a clinic. Then we went to Paris, hoping that his former artistic surroundings would stimulate him into consciousness. But nothing seemed to work. Instead, his condition gradually became worse, he slipped further and further away from reality, and we eventually returned once again to Switzerland. . . . During this period I had ample time to meditate, and I realized that it was my duty to the history of art and to Nijinsky himself to let the world know that he was more than a great dancer. Shortly after our marriage, my husband had asked me to annotate his artistic ideas, as he hoped to help the students of dancing with them. And I began to write what later became Nijinsky's biography.

When I had written my husband's biography, I wanted to recapture his art for future centuries, to reconstruct all that was in him. I tried, in my own humble way, to fix every event, every fact, and to give a true picture of Nijinsky, his life, his art, and all those who came in contact with him. The world has felt the frankness and truthfulness of my books and has accorded them an enthusiastic reception for which I am deeply grateful.

On a recent visit to Russia, I had the opportunity to meet and talk with many people: artists, students and others. Everywhere I went I found that my husband was remembered with great admiration and respect by the artists and laymen alike. His name is revered by the young students of the dance, to whom he serves as an inspiration. His fellow countrymen know that he was not a deserter like so many others who denounced and left Russia for their own personal gain. It was only because of the circumstances of the war and his illness that Nijinsky was prevented from returning to his homeland as he had planned. It was there that he had intended to establish his academy of the dance.

An immense amount has been written on Nijinsky's art as a dancer and choreographer. Nijinsky has a greater claim to fame than any dancer, which is derived from his achievements in the interpretive sphere, but it is in the domain of choreographic art that his chief honour will ever rest. With unerring taste and infallible judgment he revolutionized the art of choreography, by establishing the modern style—that of the twentieth century—in his ballets Afternoon of a Faun and The Rite of Spring.

The Diary of Nijinsky is not only a rare human document; it is unique. It allows an insight into the inner life of a creative artist—a genius. His great gentleness, his tolerance towards others, his mystic thought, his passionate love of peace and God are embodied in his diary. It permits us to follow his feelings, his thoughts, between the two worlds—the rational and the irrational.

Great men such as Nietzsche and Van Gogh went through a similar agony when from the creative visionary state of mind they perished into the world of unreality. But neither of them has written down an account of his transition as Nijinsky did in his Diary.

Now, nearly two decades after his death, I am giving you this Diary again in the hope that it will be of interest to many and will help, as a textbook for students of psychiatry, to shed some light on the beautiful mystery of the mind *and heart of Nijinsky.*

There are many who can speak about Nijinsky as an artist an dancer—only three people have or had the right and the authority to speak of his private life. They are Diaghilev and my husband, both now unfortunately dead, and myself. I have told you in my books on my husband all I had to say. Now I give you the words of Nijinsky himself.

Romola Nijinsky

San Francisco
April 1967

PART ONE

ONE

LIFE

PEOPLE WILL SAY that Nijinsky pretends to be mad on account of his bad deeds. Bad deeds are terrible and I hate them, and do not want to commit any. I made mistakes before because I did not understand God. I felt Him but did not understand what everyone was doing. Every person has "feeling"* but they do not understand what it is. I want to write this book in order to explain what feeling is. Many will say that these are my opinions only, but I know that my point of view is the right one, because it comes from God. God is in me. I have made mistakes but I corrected them with my life. I suffered more than anyone else in the world.

I invited some friends for a drive to Maloja, several miles from St. Moritz. It is a lovely drive if the weather is fine. I love nature, especially Russian nature, as I was brought up in Russia. I love Russia. My wife is frightened of Russia. It is all the same to

*When Nijinsky refers to "feeling" he means the instinct—the urge of the unconscious mind.

me where I live. I live where God wishes. I will travel all my life if God wishes. I have drawn a picture of Christ without mustaches and beard, with long hair. I look like Him, only He has a calm gaze, and my eyes look round. I am a man, of *motion*, not one of immobility. I have different habits from Christ. He loved immobility, and I love motion and dancing.

I was at little Kyra's* yesterday. She was choking with bronchitis. I do not know why they give her an inhaling machine with medicine. I am against all drugs. I don't want people to take them. Medicine is an invented thing. I know people who make a habit of taking it. People think it is a necessary thing. Medicine is useful only as a help, but it is only Nature which can give and restore health. Tolstoy did not like medicine either. I like it when it is necessary. I have said that it is useless. I said the truth because it is so. If you do not believe me—all right. I believe God and therefore write everything He tells me.

My wife told me that everything I did† at last night's party was like a spiritualist. I told her that I did not sway as mediums do, in spiritualistic seances. People in a spiritualistic trance are like drunken peo-

---

*Kyra, Nijinsky's daughter, has been staying at a neighboring house, on account of Nijinsky's nervous condition.

†N. is referring to spiritualistic seances, which are described in Romola Nijinska's NIJINSKY, chapter XIX.

ple, and I was not drunk because I knew what I was
doing. I am not a drunkard but I know what drunk-
enness is because I have drunk wines and got drunk.
I don't want people to drink and to have spiritualistic seances. It is bad for the health.

I want to speak of Nietzsche and of Darwin because they were men of thought. Darwin believed
that men descended from monkeys. He thought that
he had discovered a new theory. I asked my wife this
morning about Darwin and Nietzsche, as I was sorry
for Nietzsche. I like him. He would have understood
me. Darwin's theory of Nature is false. He did not
feel Nature. Nature is life and life is Nature. I love
it, and know what it is. I understand it because I feel
it and Nature feels me. Nature is God and I am Nature. I am alive. Nature is a wonderful thing. I know
that it will help me to study it. But I study it only
through feeling. Feeling is great and therefore I know
what nature is. Monkeys are a part of Nature, so are
men, but a monkey has not the nature of man. I feel
movement. I move simply, but the movements of a
monkey are complicated. A monkey is stupid. I am
stupid too but I have sense. I am a sensible being
and a monkey is a senseless being. Man comes from
God. God is not a monkey. Man is God. A man has
arms, so has a monkey. I know that organically a
man resembles a monkey, but spiritually he does not.

[5]

Monkeys come from Monkey, and monkeys were created by God. God came from God. I am a man descended from God and not from a monkey. I am God if I feel Him. I know that many will admire me, and this will make me happy as my aim will have been achieved.

I will dance in order to earn money. I want to give my wife a house complete with everything. She wants to have a child, reincarnation of me, as she is afraid that I will soon die. She thinks I am mad—she has this idea because she thinks too much. I think little and therefore understand everything I feel. I am feeling through the flesh and not through the intellect. I am the flesh. I am the feeling. I am God in flesh and feeling. I am man and not God. I am simple. I need not think. I must make myself felt and understood through feeling. Scientists think about me and break their heads, but their thinking will not give any results. They are stupid. I speak simply without any tricks.

The world was made by God. Man was made by God. It is impossible for man to understand God, but God understands God. Man is part of God and therefore sometimes understands God. I am both God and man. I am good and not a beast. I am an animal with a mind. I am flesh but I do come from flesh. God made flesh. I am God. I am God. I am God. . . .

[6]

Life

I am happy because I am love. I love God and therefore smile to myself. People think that I will go mad and lose my reason. Nietzsche lost his reason because he thought too much. I do not think and therefore cannot go mad. My scalp is strong and hard. I have to stand on my head in the ballet Scheherazade, in which I represent a fatally wounded negro. I portrayed him well and the public therefore understood me. Now I will express feeling and the public will understand me. I know the public because I studied them well. They like to be astonished, but they know little about Art, therefore are easily amazed. I know how to astonish the public and am therefore sure of success.

I want to have millions in order to make the Stock Exchange tremble. I want to ruin the Stock Exchange. I am life and life is love of people for one another. The Stock Exchange is death. It robs poor people who bring it their last money in the hope of realizing their ambitions. I like the poor and will therefore play on the Stock Exchange in order to ruin the brokers. The brokers play with enormous sums. Enormous sums are death and therefore not from God. I want to make money on the Stock Exchange and will therefore go to Zurich.

My wife wants me to go to Zurich to see a specialist for nerves, in order to have my nervous system examined. I promised her 100,000 francs if she is right about my nerves being in a bad way. I will give it to her if the doctor says that I have bad nerves. If she loses I will not pay her. I have not got this money now, but I have promised it to her. I will play on the Exchange, but for that reason I will have to stay several weeks in Zurich. I will go there within the next few days. I have no money and hope my wife will give me some. I will go with her. She will take me with her own money. I have a little in the bank, about 200 frs. I will play with them. I want to lose my last money that they may give me some more. God will help me to win and I am not afraid. He wants me to break the Stock Exchange. I will have money from that and not from my dancing. I will look at the papers and will buy some stocks. I do not understand German but will understand what I have to.

This morning before lunch I went to Hanselmann. I took a glass of port and lost consciousness because God so willed. I did not want to behave stupidly because I consider that death.

*I cannot force my wife to become a vegetarian. She eats meat because she loves it. At lunch I broke a nut suddenly with the force of a giant. I am very

---

The following incidents have been described in NIJINSKY, chapter XIX.

[8]

strong, having a strong fist. She got frightened and said that I struck on purpose. She was right because I did strike on purpose. She feels me better now. I pretended to be ill from the wine I had drunk before lunch—one small glass taken with a pastry! I felt giddy later. I walked out into the street with A.* and walked a few steps. I felt very limp and my knees were giving way. I almost fell and A. was very pleased with me. She loves drunken people. I know her habits. She loves her husband—they drink together. God wanted me to understand A. Yesterday she came for a walk with me because she wanted me to buy her some shoes. I gave her a pair of shoes today as she had none. I have shoes and don't need anymore. I gave her mine as they fit her. My feet are slightly bigger than hers. She does not feel me when I talk to her.

At every opportunity I tell my wife, "It is bad to eat meat." My wife understands me but does not want to eat only vegetables, thinking that it is only a whim of mine. I wished her good when I asked her not to eat sausage at night, knowing its action. She says, "What is good for you is not good for me." She does not understand me when I say that one must always do what one feels to be right. She thinks too much, and therefore has not enough feeling. I am

A. A Russian friend.

not afraid of her leaving me but I will not marry again. I love her very much and will therefore ask her forgiveness if God so wills. God does not want me to do so as He does not want her to eat meat. I gave all the money to my wife, and I often told her that if we did not eat meat we would economize more. She listened to me but did not do what I asked her. She loves me and is therefore afraid for my health. I told her that if she does not like all I do, we can get divorced and I will find her a good husband and a rich one. I told her that I could not go on living like this though my patience is great. I got nervous at the command of God and therefore hit the nut with my fist. My wife got frightened and was very nervous and therefore I went away to write.

Romola is my wife's name. It is an Italian name. She was named so by her father, a man of great mind who loved the Italy of the Renaissance. I do not like the bygone centuries because I am alive. This fountain pen I am writing with was given to me by my wife for Christmas. This yearly feast is called Christmas all over the world where there are Christians.

Today I wore the small cross which Emma had given me. Emma is my wife's mother. She loves me and Kyra too, and thinks that she proves her affection by making presents. She thinks that love is in presents. I think that a present is not the expression of love. It is a habit. One should give presents to poor people and not to those who have possessions. Kyra has enough and therefore does not need any presents. I give Kyra enough because I earn through dancing. Emma does not understand the value of money and therefore throws it about. She knows that I understand her and she therefore loves me. I would prefer her to give presents to people who need them. *Emilia is a good woman, she loves the poor and gives them a lot. I don't think it is enough to give a lot. One should permanently help the poor. One should seek out the poor and not give to the charitable institutions. I will dance for institutions only because it makes it possible for me to express my personality. I want to be a personality for the purpose of fulfilling my task. My task is the task of God and I therefore want to do everything to fulfill it. I write because God orders me to. I do not want to earn money through the writing of this book. I do not want to become rich, but God wants me to be rich because He knows my aims. I do not love money —I love people. People will understand me after I have provided them with the means of existence. Poor people cannot earn. Rich people must help them. It will be of no help if I give all my earnings

Emma or Emilia is used for the same person.

to institutions for the poor. These institutions enrich themselves and do not even think of organizing help. A poor man does not go to these charitable institutions, because he is ashamed of being misunderstood. The poor like presents given simply. I give very simply without making a fuss of it. I do not talk of Christ when I give a present. I run away from the poor when they want to thank me. I hate gratitude. I do not give because I want gratitude. I give because I love God. I am His present. I am God, in a present. I love God, and God wants me to give presents because I know how to give them. I will not go like Christ from house to house, I will meet people and they will invite me to their homes. I will study their families and will help them in every way. Money is a means of helping but is not help in itself. I will not give money because a poor man does not always know how to use it. A. is poor. She has no clothes. I try all sorts of shrewd tricks in order to help her.

She tells my wife stupid things in Hungarian and I understand Hungarian. Hungarian is a simple language and is therefore easily understood by a man with feeling. To understand does not mean to know all the words. I understand in every language. I know few words but my sense is keenly developed. I like developing my sense, because I must understand everything that is being said.

Life

I will pretend to be dying, or ill, in order to enter the cottage of the poor. I smell out the poor like a dog scenting out game. I smell very well. I will find the poor without their advertisements. I need no advertisements. I will go by scent. I will not be mistaken. I will not give money to the poor, I will give them life. Life is not poverty. Poverty is not life. I want life. I want love.

I feel that my wife is afraid of me because her movements were determined when I asked her to give me some ink. She felt cold and I too. I am afraid of the cold because it is death. I will write quickly because I am not given much time. I would very much like Kostrovsky* to help me because he understands me. I would speak and he would write and in this way we could do something else as well. I can write and think of something else. I am God in man. I feel what Christ felt. I am like Buddha. I am the Buddhist God and every kind of God. I know each of them. I have met them all. I pretend to be mad on purpose, for my own aims. I know that if everyone thinks that I am a harmless madman they will not be afraid of me. I do not like people who think that I am a dangerous lunatic. I am a madman who loves mankind. *My madness is my love towards mankind.*

---

*Kostrovsky was Nijinsky's friend, a Tolstoyan, who tried to influence him greatly. He was epileptic and died insane.

I told my wife that I had invented a pen which will make us a lot of money, but she does not believe me because she thinks that I do not understand what I am doing. I showed her the pen and a pencil, to explain my invention. I will send it to Steinhardt, my lawyer and friend, and will ask him to patent it. Steinhardt is a clever man and will therefore understand the importance of my invention. I want to sell my patent. If they will agree, I will sell it. If they don't, I will destroy it.

I am not rich and do not want riches. I want love and therefore want to throw aside all sordid money —dirt. I will give life to the poor. They will not die of hunger. I won't starve either because I know what to do in order to prevent this.

I am not a child prodigy to be exhibited—I am a sensible man. Millions of years have gone by since the creation of man. Men think that God is where technical inventions are most advanced. God was already there when there was no mechanism. Steel is a necessary thing, but it is also a terrible thing. An aeroplane is a terrible thing. I flew in an aeroplane and cried in it. I do not know why, but I felt that aeroplanes destroy birds. All birds fly away at the sight of an aeroplane. An aeroplane is a useful thing but it must not be exaggerated. It is a thing coming from God and therefore I like it, but it must not be used for the purposes of war. An aeroplane should express goodwill. I like aeroplanes and will therefore fly in them where there are no birds. I love birds. I do not want to frighten them. A well-known flyer was flying in Switzerland and flew into an eagle. The eagle is savage and does not like other birds, but one must not kill him because God gave him life.

I went to two schools in Petersburg, where they taught me enough. I did not need a university education as it was not necessary for me to know a great deal.

I do not like universities because they spend their time on politics. Politics are death. Politics are invented by the governments. Men have lost their way and cannot understand each other and have therefore divided themselves into parties. I forgot about the aeroplane which hit an eagle. The eagle is a bird of God and one must not kill tsars, emperors, and kings. I like tsars and the aristocrats, but their deeds are not always good deeds. I will give them a good example, by not destroying them. I will help them in every way because I love God, but I beg everyone to help me in this, because, alone I cannot do everything God wants. I want everyone to help me and they must all come to me for help. I am God and my address is in God. I do not live in the streets, I live in men. I want to work on the feelings of men. I love simple feeling which everyone has. I do not want people with bad feelings.

War has not stopped through the thinking of men. I know how one could stop war. Wilson wants to stop war but men do not understand him. He wants tolerance in politics, therefore he does not like war. He did not want war.

Lloyd George is a simple man, but he has a great brain. But his brain destroys feeling and therefore he has no wisdom in politics. Lloyd George is a difficult man. Diaghilev is a terrible man. I do not like terrible men, but I will not harm them. I do not want them to be killed. They are eagles. They prevent small birds from living, and therefore one must be on one's guard against them. I like them because God gave them life and He has a right to their existence. I am not to be their judge, but God, but I will tell them the truth. By saying the truth I destroy the evil which they have done. I know that Lloyd George does not like people who are in his way. Diaghilev neither. Diaghilev is smaller than Lloyd George but he is also an eagle. An eagle must not interfere with the smaller birds and must therefore be given enough to eat in order not to attack them. Diaghilev is a bad man and loves boys. One must stop men like him by any means, from going on with their deeds. One must not lock them up though. They must not suffer. "Christ is not Antichrist," as Merejkovski said. Dostoievsky wrote about a stick with two ends. Tolstoy talked about a tree which had roots and branches. A branch is not a root and a root is not a branch. I like roots because they are useful. Christ is God, Antichrist is not God. I don't like Antichrist because he is not God. Antichrist no longer exists, like things in the museums and history. I do not like history or museums, because they are like cemeteries. Dostoievsky was a great writer who described his life under the guise of different personalities.

People go to church to look for God. God is not in the church. He is in churches and everywhere where we seek him and I will therefore go to church, too. I do not like the church because one does not speak of God there, one speaks of learning. Learning is not God. God is wisdom and learning is Antichrist. I speak strongly on purpose in order to be better understood, and not in order to hurt people. People will be offended because they will think and not feel. I know the whole world is contaminated with rottenness which rots away, even trees. The tree of Tolstoy is life and therefore we must read him. I know his *Anna Karenina*, but I have forgotten it a little. I have also read *War and Peace*. Tolstoy is a great man and writer. He was ashamed of his writing in later years, when he thought he was nearer God. I like journalists who like people, they are understanding, even those who are obliged to write nonsense for money. Merejkovski writes beautifully. P.H. writes cleverly. I know about the controversy between P.H. [Phil] and a magazine which was called the *New Times.** Phil did not understand Merejkovski. Merejkovski looked for God and did not find him.

I would prefer my writing to be photographed instead of printed, because printing does away with handwriting. Handwriting is a lovely thing; it is alive and full of character. I want my handwriting to be photographed because I want people to understand it as it comes from God. I could write beautifully but do not want to be perfect. I am not an aristocrat. I come from the people. I love the aristocrats but I want love for all people. I love my servants, and I love my wife. I understand my wife. She likes good manners. I am not polite in my manners because I do not want to be. My love is simple.

I know that if a man who can analyze handwritings reads this, he will say that "the writer is an unusual man," because the handwriting jumps. I know that jerky handwriting means kindness of heart. I am able to tell good people from their handwriting.

---

*Novoye Vremia, *one of the important daily newspapers of St. Petersburg before the revolution.*

Diaghilev is a bad man, but I know how to beware of his nastiness. He thinks that my wife has all the brains and therefore is afraid of her. He is not afraid of me because I used to behave nervously. He does not like highly-strung people, but he is nervous as he is always stimulating himself to excitement, as well as his friends.

Z., his friend, is a very good man but a bore. His aim is simple. He wants to become rich and learn everything that Diaghilev knows. Z. knows nothing. D. thinks that he is the God of Art. I want to challenge him so that the whole world shall see. I want to show that all Diaghilev's art is utter nonsense. I will help people to understand Diaghilev. I worked with him for five years without rest. I know all his sly tricks and habits. I was with Diaghilev. I know him better than he knows himself, his weak and his strong points. I am not afraid of him. He is a rich man as his parents left him a fortune. The Spaniards spill the blood of bulls and therefore like murder. They are terrible people because they murder bulls. Even the Church and the Pope cannot put an end to this slaughter. The Spaniards think that a bull is a beast. The toreador weeps before killing the bull. I know many toreadors whose stomachs the bull has split. I hated this slaughter but I was not understood. Diaghilev said with Z. that a bullfight is a magnificent art. I know that they both will say that I am mad and one cannot be offended with me, because D. always used that trick; he thinks that no one understands him. I understand him and therefore challenge him to a bullfight. I am the bull, a wounded bull. I am God in the bull. I am Apis. I am an Egyptian. I am an Indian. I am a Red Indian. I am a Negro. I am a Chinaman. I am a Japanese. I am a foreigner, a stranger. I am a sea bird. I am a land bird. I am the tree of Tolstoy. I am the roots of Tolstoy—Tolstoy is mine. I am his. Tolstoy lived in the same time as I. I loved him but did not understand him—Tolstoy is great and I was afraid of the great. The newspapers did not understand Tolstoy; he was built up like a giant in one of the magazines after his death, but only as they wanted to belittle the Tsar. The Tsar is a man like the rest of us, and therefore I did not want his death. I am sorry for the Tsar.

I love Zola although I read him very little. I know a short story of his which made me understand him. I want to read a lot of his works. I am very sad about Zola's death, because he was asphyxiated. Men killed him because they were afraid of the truth. I will be killed then, I am not afraid of death. I do not want the death of my murderer and therefore beg people, after I am killed, not to lynch or kill him, as it was not his fault. The murderer goes to death; those who start war are murderers because they kill millions of innocent people. I am a man in a million. I am not alone, because I feel more than a million others.

My family think that I do not understand what they are saying in Hungarian. I write and at the same time listen to their conversation. My writing does not prevent me from thinking of something else. I lived at my mother-in-law's during the war. Once I wanted to walk into a restaurant but an inner force kept me back. I stopped suddenly before a small res-taurant frequented by working people. I wanted to enter but I did not like to as I was not a workman. I like working people. They feel more than the rich. They are just the same as rich men, the only differ-ence being that they have little money. I saw some workmen today and therefore wanted to talk about them. They drink cheap wine.

I liked Paris cocottes when I was with Diaghilev. He thought me stupid, but I used to run to them. I ran about Paris looking for cheap cocottes, but I was afraid people would notice my actions. I know that those women have no disease as they are under special police supervision. I knew that everything I did was awful, and that if I were found out I would be lost. In those days I did many stupid things. All young men do silly things. In the streets of Paris I went in search of cocottes. I looked for a long time because I wanted the girl to be healthy and beautiful—sometimes I looked all day long and found nobody because I was inexperienced. I loved several cocottes every day. I went for walks along the boulevards and often met cocottes who did not understand me. I used to make use of all sorts of tricks in order to draw their attention, as they paid very little to me because I was simply dressed. I was dressed quietly in order not to be recognized. One day I was following a cocotte when I noticed a young man staring at me. He was in a carriage with his wife and his two children. He recognized me and I felt terribly humiliated, so I turned blushing. But I continued my chase. If my wife reads this, she will go mad because she trusts me. I lied to her, saying that she was the first woman I had known. Before my wife I knew many others. She was simple and lovely to look at.

I once loved a woman who taught me everything. I was shocked and told her that it was a pity to do things like that. She told me that if she did not do it she would die of hunger, but I said that I wanted nothing, and I gave her money. She begged me to stay, but I would not agree because I felt humiliated for her. I left her alone. I found rooms in small hotels. Paris is full of them. I know many hotels of this kind,

which exist by hiring rooms for an hour or two for
free love. I call it "free love" when men like exciting
women. I hate excitement and therefore I do not
want to eat meat. I ate meat today and felt a longing
for a streetwalker. I did not love that woman but my
desire sent me after her. I wanted to make love to
her but God held me back. I am afraid of lust because I know its meaning. It is the death of life. Men
with this urge are like beasts. I am not a beast and
therefore I turned home. On my way God stopped
me because He did not want me to go on. I suddenly
noticed the same girl with a man. She was trying to
stop him from going into a restaurant. The man
then asked her in Italian to enter the restaurant with
her girl friend. I stood there dumbfounded for a long
time—my feelings were keeping me back. After they
entered the restaurant, an elderly man shut the door,
saying good day to me. I answered the same. I had
a habit of greeting everyone, even if I did not know
them. I understood that all people were equal. I
often state, but am not always understood, that we
are all equal. By that I mean that one should love
everyone. I love my wife more than anyone in the
world. I told her that today. My wife continues to
weep in her soul, but I am not afraid of her sorrow.
I love her but I cannot give up my writing, for it is
too important for me. My wife is afraid that I am

writing unpardonable things. I laugh at her weeping, because I know its meaning. I want to soothe her, but my hand continues to write. My wife is reading what I write, looking under my hand. I will tell her that if she wants to know before everyone else she must learn Russian, but I do not really want her to learn Russian because I do not wish her to know what I am writing. I do not want any person to read it before the others. I will soon publish this book. My wife is crying because she is afraid that I will not stop. I will stop writing only if God wishes. I love my wife because she has felt what I am writing and she is afraid for me, and also afraid that if I am killed, she and the child will be left alone in this world.

*Romuska's mother is a difficult woman. I love her but I know that if she finds out that I have no money she will cast me off.

She discusses matters with her husband in the evening. She likes to think at night. I know her habits because I have lived in the same house. She loves me because she knows that I am a celebrity. I do not like celebrities. I want her to think that I am mad in order to have the opportunity of studying her. I like her but I know her ways. She has a good heart but often quarrels with her husband. My wife suffered a great deal because of her mother when

---

Romuska is the diminutive for Romola.

we lived with them. I also suffered on account of my wife's sufferings. I know that some people will say that this is not true because my mother-in-law kisses my wife and me and the little one. She can pretend because she is an actress, and I know that her acting has no feeling, it is all pretense. I talked of her kindness because I do not want people to think that I am nasty.

I do not pretend and I write the truth. One day I hurt Louise, the maid, but afterwards I was so pained that I found no peace anywhere.

My wife put matters right. She told Louise that I was nervous and that I did not mean to hurt her, and the maid came to me, very ashamed, and asked my forgiveness. I gave her my hand and told her that I love her. She understood me and since then we like each other.

I love my wife and do not wish her any harm and will therefore go and earn money in order to make her happy. I do not want her to suffer and would like to earn enough for her to live on if I were to be killed. I am not afraid of death, but my wife is. She thinks that death is an awful thing. Mental agony *is* a terrible thing, but I want people to understand that death of the body is not.

I can no longer trust my wife, as I feel that she wants to give this diary to the doctor for examination. I said that no one had the right to touch my books. I do not want people to see them so I hid them, and this part I am going to carry on me. I will hide my notes as people do not like the truth. I am afraid of people, as I think they will hurt me. But I will go on loving them even if they do hurt me as they are creations of God's. I love my wife and she loves me, but believes in the doctors. I know doctors, I understand them. They want to examine my brain, but I want to examine their minds. But they cannot examine my brain, for they have not seen it. I wrote some poetry*in order that the doctors could observe the working of my brain. I wrote sensibly, but they asked senseless questions. My answers were quick and to the point. They did not want to accept one of the poems, for they did not think it was important from the psychological point of view. They did all this on purpose, thinking that I did not know what I was doing, but I know everything I do and therefore I am not afraid. I pretend on purpose to be mad, in order to be put into an asylum. I know that A. telephoned the doctor about me, but I am not afraid of them. I know the love of my wife. She will not leave me. She is afraid of me, but she will never leave me. I am terrified of being locked up and of losing my work.

Nijinsky refers to an association test.

I do not want death of the senses, I want people to understand. I cannot cry and shed tears over what I write, but I cry within me. I am sad. I love every-one. I write quickly but clearly. I know that people usually like my writing.

I want Wilson to succeed in his undertakings, be-cause they are near the truth. I feel the near death of Wilson. I was afraid for Clemenceau, too, because Clemenceau is a good man. His policy is stupid and therefore his life hangs on a hair. Men feel his mis-takes. He is not aware of this and therefore his life is in danger. I love Clemenceau, because he is a child. I know children who do awful things, without wanting to. Lloyd George does not know that he will be found out, and therefore holds his head very high. I want to lower his head. I like him, but I must write the truth. I know that if he reads these notes, he will understand me. I know that Clemenceau is honest; he is the policy of France. He is a hard-working man, but he was mistaken when he sent France to her death. He is a man who seeks good-ness, a child with a tremendous brain. Some poli-ticians are hypocrites like Diaghilev, who does not want universal love, but to be loved alone. I want universal love.

I want to dance for the benefit of the poor in France. I am of Polish descent, but I am Russian at heart because I was brought up in Russia. I love

Russia. Paderewski became a politician but he is a pianist. I like pianists who play with feeling. Music with feeling is Godlike. I do not like pure technique without feeling. I know people will disagree and will say that Paderewski is a musician with feeling. I do not like politics, and I detest politicians who seek to enlarge the frontiers of a country. I like a policy whose aim it is to keep the country from war.

I will tell the whole truth, and others will continue what I have begun. I am like Zola, but I want to speak and not write novels. Novels prevent one from understanding feelings. I seek truth in a book and not the subject. I do not like disguise. It is hypocritical. Criminals ought not to be put into prison or killed. They are not terrible and I am not afraid of them. During the World War every man was a criminal. The governments shielded the criminals, because the crimes of the governments were executed by them. God does not shield a government which wages war. He does not want war and has therefore sent horrors on mankind. I am myself a criminal, because I kill the mind. I do not want thought, I want wisdom. I am God. I am Love. I want to write a letter to the doctor. I will write it in this notebook and not on writing paper:

"My dear friend, I have hurt you; but I did not mean to hurt you as I love you. I wish you good and therefore pretend to be mad. I wanted you to feel what I was thinking and feeling, but you failed, as you thought that I was mad. I pretended to be a very nervous man in order that you should feel that I was *not* nervous. I am a man who disguises his feelings. I do not wish any harm to my wife, I love her. I love you. I am Christ's policy. I am Christ. I hate ridicule. I am *not* funny. I love everyone and there is nothing ridiculous in loving everyone. I know you. You have feeling. You do not like things that are not calm, because you have weak nerves. I on the other hand have strong nerves. I am not trying to start a campaign for the extermination of nervous people. I do not like propaganda. You are a German. You were born in Switzerland, but your education is German. I love the Germans. You must heal without money, because you are rich. I understand you. You want to give your wife everything to make her happy, but you forget that there are many suffering people. You say that you love Germany. I also. You are rich, but you do not give money to poor Germans. They are dying of starvation. I know that you will say that Switzerland cannot help the Germans, because it has little itself. I quite understand the position of Switzerland. It is between two fires. Both fires are terrible. I detest the fire that destroys life and like only that which gives warmth. One need not form organizations in order to govern or lead. Love will destroy the need for governing. I like the leadership of Wilson. I do not want my wife to die. I love her. I acted badly in order that you should help me. I know that my wife is nervous because of my action, and that I will be forced to go away. My trunks are already packed. Disaster is a terrible thing. I will ask my wife's forgiveness when you tell me to. I want you to heal my wife, but I cannot be healed. I do not want to be healed. I am not afraid of anything except the death of wisdom. I want the death of the mind. My wife will not go mad if I kill her mind. The mind is stupidity, but wisdom is God. You think that because I build everything on feeling, I have lost my mind. A man who bases everything on feeling is not horrible, and I do not want bad feelings and will therefore go and kiss my wife, and say that God tells me to. I am not afraid of you. You will be my dearest friend and understand me. I also want to help you."

I will remain alone, and cry in my loneliness. I cry a lot, but will not give up writing. I am afraid that Doctor X., my friend, will come in and see my tears, and as I do not want to upset him, I will wipe them away. I cry in such a way as not to interfere with anyone. A. thinks that I am pretending, but I am not. I will go to my wife after A. has left. I do not want a scene, loving peace. I will not cry now, be-

Nijinsky practising on American tour (1916)

Nijinsky in uniform at 18

Nijinsky at school

cause everyone will feel sorry for me. I do not want
people to pity me, but to be loved. I did not go to
see A. off, because God does not want me to stop
writing. I kissed her, writing these words. She saw
my tears, but did not see my weakness. I pretended
to be weak, because that was God's wish. I understand the love of my people, who do not want to leave
my wife alone. I am poor. I have nothing and I want
nothing. I am not crying, but have tears in my heart.
I do not wish any harm to my wife, I love her more
than anyone else, and know that if we parted I would
die. I cry . . . I cannot restrain my tears, and they fall
on my left hand and on my silken tie, but I cannot
and do not want to hold them back. I feel that I am
doomed. I do not want to go under. I do not know
what I need, and I dislike to upset my people. If they
are upset, I will die. I love Louise and Marie.* Marie
prepares me food and Louise serves it. I want to
sleep, but my wife does not feel me. She thinks in her
dreams; I do not, and therefore will not go to sleep.
I cannot sleep because of the powders. They give me
all sorts of powders, but I cannot sleep. If they were
to inject morphia, I would not sleep either. I know
myself; my wife took a sleeping draught and therefore has a heavy head. The doctor wants her to sleep.

Louise was the maid, Marie the cook in the Nijinsky household.

She will have a long sleep, but she will not die. She will live. Her death has already arrived, because she does not have any faith in the doctor. In spite of the powder she cannot sleep. I stayed a long time with her. I sat, I sat a long time, then I pretended to fall asleep. I pretended because I felt that way. Whenever I have a feeling I carry it out. I never fight against a feeling. An order of God tells me how to act. I am not a fakir and a magician. I am God in a body. Everyone has that feeling, but no one uses it. I do make use of it, and know its results. People think that this feeling is a spiritual trance, but I am not in a trance. I am love. I am in a trance, the trance of love. I want to say so much and cannot find the words. I want to write and cannot. I can write in a trance, and this trance is called *wisdom*. Every man is a reasonable being. I do not want unreasonable beings and therefore I want everyone to be in a trance of feelings. I am in a trance of God. God wants me to sleep. People will say that all that I write is stupid, but in reality it has a deep meaning.

Once in the mountains I came to a road which led up to a peak. I climbed up and stopped. I wanted to make a speech on the mountain; I felt a wish to do so, but I did not because I thought that everyone would say that I was mad. I was not. I had a great wish to speak. I felt no pain, but a great love towards

[32]

the people. I wanted to shout from the top of the mountain into the village of St. Moritz. I did not because I felt I had to continue my way. I went on and came to a tree. The tree told me that one could not talk here, because human beings do not understand feeling. I went on. I was sorry to part with the tree, because the tree understood me. I walked. I climbed up 2,000 meters—stood there a long time. I felt a voice and shouted in French: "*Parole!*" I wanted to speak, but my voice was so strong, that I could only shout: "I love everyone! I want happiness! I love everyone! I want everyone!" I want to love everyone and be understood, and therefore want to speak all languages but cannot, therefore I write, and my writings will be translated.

I went for a walk and thought of Christ. I am a Christian—a Catholic, a Russian. My daughter does not speak Russian, because the war prevented us from going to Russia. My little one sings in Russian, because I taught her Russian songs. I love them and the Russian language. I know many Russians, who are not really so in their heart, but always use foreign languages. I love Russia. I love France. I love England. I love America. I love Switzerland. I love Spain. I love Italy. I love Japan. I love Australia. I love China. I love Africa. I love the Transvaal. I want to love everyone and therefore I am like God.

I am neither Russian nor Pole. I am a man. I am not a foreigner or a cosmopolitan. I love the Russian soil. *I will build a dam in Russia.* I understand Gogol loved Russia. So do I. Russia feels more than any other country. She is the mother of all countries, and loves everyone. Russia is not a problem of politics. I know that many people in Russia will understand me. Russia is not Bolshevik. Russia is my mother. I love my mother. My mother lives in Russia. She is Polish, but she eats Russian bread and *Schzi*.* I want love for my Russia although I know her shortcomings. She has destroyed the plan of war. The war would have ended earlier if she had not let in the Maximalists. The Russian people are like children. One must love them and govern them well.

If everyone will listen to me, there will be no more war. I do not like parties, but democracy is the best among them, because everybody has the same rights. I do not really like rights at all, as nobody has any rights in reality. I do not want the laws of man—they are invented. Napoleon created laws and his were better than others; but it does not mean that these were the laws of God. People will say that one cannot live without laws, because men kill each other. I know that men have not yet arrived at loving each other,

---

**Sour cabbage soup.*

but they will love each other. I have gone to law many a time. I had lawsuits against Diaghilev and I won them, because I was right. I know that Diaghilev hoped to win. My lawyer is one of the best, but he will lose my lawsuit, because my friend, the Marchioness of R., has died. He hoped that she would take him under her wing. I know that he could win the lawsuit, if I gave him a lot of money, but I do not know anything about business and therefore am afraid to entrust my lawsuit to him. I like him, but I do not trust him, because he is dragging the case out. I feel that I was right in winning the Diaghilev lawsuit. I do not want money from Diaghilev which I have not earned. He does not want me to pay when the work I did for him has cost me my life. There is an English doctor who can witness this, as can my wife. According to law, she has no right to testify, but I will go to court in such a way that she will have every right to. I know God will help me.

I like to speak in rhymes, because I am a rhyme myself. I went for a walk, but met no friends.

My wife sighs because she thinks that I am writing about politics. She wants to see, but I will not let her, and cover up my writings with my hand.

One evening I went for a walk up the hill, and stopped on the mountain . . . "the mountain of

Sinai."* I was cold. I had walked far. Feeling that I should kneel, I quickly knelt and then felt that I should put my hand on the snow. After doing this, I suddenly felt a pain and cried with it, pulling my hand away. I looked at a star, which did not say good evening to me. It did not twinkle at me. I got frightened and wanted to run, but could not, because my knees were rooted to the snow. I started to cry, but no one heard my weeping. No one came to my rescue. I loved going for walks but felt a terror. I did not know what to do and could find no reason for my slowness. After several minutes I turned and saw a house. It was closed and the windows shuttered. A little further away there was another house the roof of which was covered with ice. I felt frightened and shouted at the top of my voice: "Death!" I do not know why, but felt that one must shout "Death!" After that I felt warmer and the warmth in my body helped me to get up. Rising, I walked towards the house, where a lamp was burning. The house was big. I was not frightened of entering, but *thought* one should not enter, and therefore went past. When people get tired they need help and I wanted help, because I felt very tired. I could not walk further, but suddenly felt a tremendous force in me and ran, but

Nijinsky means it symbolically.

not for a long time. I ran until I felt the cold. The frost hit me in the face and I was frightened. The wind was blowing from the south, and I knew that the southern wind would bring more snow. I walked on the snow which crunched beneath my feet. I liked the snow and listened to its crunching. I loved listening to my footsteps; they were full of life. Looking at the sky, I saw the stars which were twinkling at me and felt merriness in them. I was happy and no long felt cold. I started walking quickly, because I saw a small wood where the trees were leafless. I felt cold, looking at the stars, seeing one that did not move. I started to go down a dark road, walking quickly, but was stopped by a tree which saved me. I was on the edge of a precipice. I thanked the tree. It felt me because I caught hold of it; it received my warmth and I received the warmth of the tree. I do not know who most needed the warmth. I walked on and suddenly stopped, seeing a precipice without a tree. I understood that God had stopped me because He loves me, and therefore said: "*If it is Thy will, I will fall down the precipice. If it is Thy will, I will be saved.*" Then I felt that I was being pushed forward but did not fall down. God loves me—I knew that all that is good is God and therefore was sure that God did not want my death. I walked on quickly down the hill and passed a hotel. Christ also went for walks. My walks were with God. Passing the hotel, I felt tears, understanding that the whole life in places like this is like death. Mankind makes merry and God mourns. It is not the fault of mankind.

My wife thinks a lot but feels little, and started to weep, so that my throat swelled with tears and I wept, covering my face with my hands. I was not ashamed but felt sad and was afraid for my wife. Wishing her good, I did not know what to do. The whole life of my wife and of all mankind is death. I was shocked and thought how lovely it would be, if my wife were to listen to me. My wife leads a good life, Stravinsky also leads a good life. Igor Stravinsky does not know what life is, he does not love me. Igor thinks that I am against his aims. He seeks riches and glory. I do not want these. Stravinsky is a good composer, but he does not think about life. His compositions have no purpose. I do not like works of art that have no moral aim. I often explained this to him, and what my idea is, but he thought that I was a stupid boy and therefore talked only to Diaghilev, who agreed with his ideas. I could say nothing, because I was supposed to be a youngster. Stravinsky's father was a Russian and his uncle a Pole. Stravinsky smells things out. He is not my friend, but at the bottom of his heart he loves me, because he feels me, but he considers me his enemy because I am in his way. Diaghilev loves Massine and not me and that is awkward for Stravinsky. Stravinsky forces his wife to carry out all his caprices. He will say that I have not seen their life together, and therefore cannot discuss it. His wife loves him. I feel that he does not love her as much, but he does love the children. He loves his children strangely and shows his love for them by making them paint; they paint well. He is like an emperor and his children and wife are the servants and soldiers. Stravinsky reminds me of Tsar Paul, but he will not be strangled because he is cleverer than the Tsar was. Diaghilev wanted to strangle him many a time,* but Stravinsky is so sly. He cannot exist without Stravinsky, and Stravinsky cannot live without Diaghilev. Both understand each other. Stravinsky fights with Diaghilev very cleverly. I know both their tricks. Once—it was after my liberation from Hungary—I went to Morges to see Stravinsky and asked him, being absolutely sure that my wish would not be refused, if he and his wife would take my child while we were in America. Knowing that he had many children I felt that my Kyra would be safe with them. I did not want to take my little one with me but wanted to leave her in the hands of another loving mother. I asked Stravinsky to take my Kyra. His wife almost wept and Stravinsky said that he was

Nijinsky means this symbolically.

very sorry, but he could not take the child, being afraid of the responsibility. I thanked him and did not say anything else to him. Looking at his wife sadly I felt the same answer. She said nothing, but by my silent tears she felt me. Being a woman, she knew what it means to drag a child from trains to steamer, from place to place, and she was sorry for me. She did not agree with her husband, but because he spoke so quickly and decisively he made her understand that he did not wish to keep my daughter. I told him that I would pay all Kyra's expenses, but he did not want to agree with this either. He advised me when we were alone to send Kyra with a governess to a hotel, but I told him that I could not leave my child in the hands of a stranger, as I did not know if the woman would love her. I do not like people who send their children to strangers. Children should always be with their mothers.

I took my Kyra to America. Stravinsky saw me off at the station, and I gave him my hand very coldly. I did not like him then, and therefore wanted to show him this, but he did not feel it because he kissed me. I had a nasty feeling.

We stayed in America for a year and a half. Thinking that traveling with the child would be bad for her, I left her in New York. Stravinsky did not write

to me, nor I to him. Already almost a year and a half
I have heard nothing of him. Stravinsky is a dry man.

My wife received a telegram. I do not know what
she is thinking, but she loves me. My Romuska loves,
but she will not understand me. My feelings are good.
What I say is sincere. God helps me. I love God. He
loves me. I know that everyone has forgotten what
God is. Everyone thinks it is a lie. The scientists say
there is no God, but I say that there is a God. I feel
Him. I don't think— I know that mothers understand
me better than others, because they feel the nearness
of death, giving birth to a child. A mother knows that
if God is not with her, no doctor on earth can save
her from death. Some think that people can live without God. I know that they will say that there is no
God, that everything is moving matter. People who
are ill feel the nearness of God more—they think they
will soon die. Ill people work with God without
knowing it. I work with Him too when I am healthy.
My wife believes that I am healthy and no longer
need any doctors. She believes in me, because she
saw things which a simple man cannot invent. I have
invented a new fountain pen.

I will give these notes to my wife, instead of giving
them to mankind. I would be understood much better, if I played the part of a man the same as others. I
have not long to live and therefore want quickly to

[41]

fulfill my tasks, which are the tasks of God. I do not pretend; I am the truth. If I tell the truth, the whole truth, men will kill me. I am afraid of one man. I am afraid of mankind, but pitying; I want to help them, making use of every way God shows me. God does not want suffering for my wife or mankind. I love my wife as much as I love mankind, and wish her the same happiness. People say that one must not love one person, when the whole world is suffering. But there is no need for one person to suffer for the happiness of humanity. Christ suffered and no one understood Him. Tolstoy and other writers wrote, apart from their novels, things about God. They understood His teaching partly, but were afraid of life.

My wife is afraid for me, therefore she transfers her fears to me. I am not afraid, having experienced the terror of death near a precipice. No one wanted to kill me, and a tree saved me.

When I was a boy and my father wanted to teach me to swim, he threw me into the water, I fell and sank to the bottom. I could not swim, and felt that I could not breathe. I kept the little air I had, shutting my mouth, thinking that if God wishes, I shall be saved. I do not know how I walked under the water, and suddenly saw the light. Understanding that I was walking towards shallow water, I hastened my steps and came to a straight wall. I saw no sky above me, only water. Suddenly I felt a physical strength in me and jumped, saw a cord, grasped it, and was saved. I tell everything that happened to me. You can ask my mother; if she has not forgotten this incident, she will tell you it happened in St. Petersburg on the Neva at the men's bathing establishment. I saw my father diving into the water, but I was afraid. I disliked somersaults. I was a boy of six or seven, but have not forgotten the story. I should like to create an impression on my little one, for children do not forget what happens to them. My doctor told me to be gentle with Kyra, because the child does not forget how the father and mother treat it. He told me that his father was once angry with him and he cannot even now forget his anger until today. The doctor's distorted face made me feel the offense of his father. I almost cried. I was sorry. I do not know whom to pity more, the son or the father. They both are miserable. The child had lost his love for the father and the father the love of God. My wife is telephoning. Thinking that I have gone for a walk she is having a heart-to-heart talk with the doctor. My wife loves me, she did not say anything nasty about me. She told him that I am conservative and that it is difficult to convince me, but that by and by one can change everything. She wishes me good, and therefore I will pretend to change. I will show my change in practice. I want a lot of money and will go to Zurich in order to get money for work. Everyone seems to think that playing on the Stock Exchange means work, I will gamble with my last money, there is not much left, a few hundred francs. God will help me, but I am afraid to hurt poor people. I do not want to rob small people, because they are poor. They seek happiness. I do not want to rob either poor or rich. I will win because I am with God. I showed my wife my love by not taking my notes away from her, when she wanted to return them to me. She told me to hide them. I purposely said that she ought to hide them, as they might be stolen from me, so she hid them. She thinks that these manuscripts would bring money. She has very little money. Everyone thinks that she has millions, but she wears imitation pearls. Noticing that people trust the rich, I gave her a ring in order that everyone should think that she is rich.

God wishes happiness for my wife and mankind. Therefore I will seek money. I do not wish this sort of happiness for myself, but through it I will give love to others. *I feel a piercing stare from behind.** I feel people want to harm me but I will not fight and my enemy will be disarmed. There are men who will

---

A visual hallucination.

beat a man to death, even if he does not answer. God
will stop them. Diaghilev and people like him will
try, but I am more and more convinced that their
efforts will remain without result. They will not kill
me. They may wound me, but will not kill me. I am
not afraid of suffering, because God will be with me.
I know how to suffer.

Lombroso made a study of skulls. I did not read
Lombroso, but I know about him from what my wife
told me. I am a madman with sense and my nerves
are trained.

I love smiling people, but not when the smile is
forced as Diaghilev's. He thinks that people do not
feel it. He does not understand the people, but wants
to be obeyed. I know a French couple in Paris, the
wife is hypocritical. Her husband is aware of this,
but he loves her. She has a child by him. I was having tea with them one day. The husband is a nice
man; there is feeling in his smile. His wife's smile is
exciting. I did not smile at her, only at her husband.
She writes letters to me, trying to explain that she
loves me. From these letters I see the slyness of that
woman.

I understood the man Diaghilev loved before me.
Diaghilev loved this man physically, therefore he
wanted to be loved in return. Diaghilev developed in
him the passion for works of art. In Massine he de-

veloped the love for glory. I was not passionate either about works of art or glory. Diaghilev noticed this and left me alone. Left alone I ran after the girls. I liked them. Diaghilev thought that I was bored, but I was not. I practiced my dances and composed ballets alone. Diaghilev did not like this. He did not want me to do things alone, but I could not agree with him. We often quarreled. I used to lock my door —our rooms were communicating—and would let in no one. I was afraid of him. I knew that all my life was in his hands. I would not leave the room. Diaghilev was also alone. He was annoyed because everyone noticed our quarrel. He hated to hear people asking, "What is the matter with Nijinsky?" Diaghilev liked to make believe that I was his pupil in everything. I did not want to agree with Diaghilev and therefore often quarreled with him in public. He went to Stravinsky for help—that was in a London hotel. Stravinsky took Diaghilev's side because he thought that Diaghilev would leave me. I felt hatred against Stravinsky as he was defending a wrong cause. I pretended to be defeated. Stravinsky thought that I was a nasty person. I was twenty-one years old, young, and often made mistakes, but I always wanted to correct them. Noticing that no one liked me, I pretended that I was disagreeable. I did not like Diaghilev, but lived with him; I hated Diaghilev

[46]

from the first days of our acquaintance, because I
knew his power. I was poor and 65 rubles* were not
enough to keep my mother and myself from starvation. We rented a flat with two rooms for 35 or 37
rubles a month.

Kyra did not want to come to see me today, because I had scolded her for being naughty. She understood, as I looked at her, that I was angry. My
wife thought that I was wrongly accusing Kyra, and
said so, in defense of the child. I answered her roughly.
I left them both alone in the room, but felt that I
had made a mistake. For I did not want Kyra to be
frightened of me. When she came in my room later,
I called her and said that if she wished she could
stay with me, but she left and I felt pain in my soul.
I did not wish her harm. She thought that I did not
love her and therefore went. I noticed a movement
of the child towards me, but I pushed her away because I thought it would be better if she left. I wanted
to call her back and went to look for her, but found
her with a nurse from the Red Cross. After a few
minutes I said that Kyra had left me as she did not
love me. The nurse almost cried, but her instinct
made her tell Kyra to say that she loved me. I was
unhappy. I did not want Kyra to suffer. I wanted to

---

*Sixty-five rubles was the monthly salary of the dancers at the Im-
perial Theater, after they graduated from the Imperial School.*

[47]

show her that I loved her, and said afterwards that I was going away from her because she did not love me. I created an impression on her. Her mother was frightened because she thought that I wanted to harm the child. I told her that I had a right to educate my child my own way. She was hurt because she felt that I had said this on purpose to discredit her, which I did not mean to do. I went downstairs and started to write down what I meant.

During luncheon I made my wife understand that I knew what they had decided with the doctor. She lied to me, as she was afraid of me. The sweet was full of medicine and therefore I left it and asked for some fruit. I know that there was medicine in the sweet, because my wife took a very small helping. I purposely took a lot, but left the sweet, pointing at it so that everyone should understand that it was nasty. The servant who entered by chance asked me, not having seen that I had pushed the sweet away, "Is it good?" I answered "Marvelous!" She felt what I had meant, seeing the sweet which had been tasted and not finished. I will not eat food with medicine in it.

I loved music. One day I met a Russian prince who introduced me to a Polish count. I have forgotten his name, because I wanted to. I do not want to hurt his whole family. This count bought me a piano.

I did not love him. I loved the prince and not the count. Ivor introduced me to Diaghilev, who asked me to come to the Hotel Europe, where he lived. I disliked him for his too self-assured voice, but went to seek my luck. I found my luck. At once I allowed him to make love to me. I trembled like a leaf. I hated him, but pretended, because I knew that my mother and I would die of hunger otherwise. I understood Diaghilev from the first moment and pretended to agree with him at once. One had to live, and therefore it was all the same to me what sort of sacrifice I had to make. I worked hard at my dancing and was always tired. But I pretended not to be tired at all in order that Diaghilev should not be bored with me. I know what he felt, he loved boys and therefore could not understand me. I do not want people to think that Diaghilev was a villain and that he should be imprisoned.* I would cry, if people were to harm him. I do not love him, but he is a human being. Loving everyone, I do not want to cause pain to anyone. Everyone will be shocked reading these lines, but I want to publish them during my lifetime, knowing their effect. I want to give the impression of something alive and true. I do not want people to read my life only after my death. I am not

*Nijinsky had Oscar Wilde's lawsuit and fate in mind.

afraid of death, but I am afraid of attacks. People will misunderstand me. I wish no harm to Diaghilev. "*I pray, leave him in peace.*" I love him the same as all other people. Not being God, I cannot judge men, God will be his judge and not the laws of man, which punish people for their mistakes. Diaghilev hurts me, not you, and I do not want to punish him. Everyone knows his mistakes. I have punished myself by telling everyone about my life. Do not think that I am writing for hypocritical reasons. If people want to punish all those about whom I have written, I will defend them. I am not writing in order to make people rise against each other. I have no right to judge. God is the judge and not the people. I am a man in God. I speak with the words of God.

I wish to explain what God is, to everyone, but I will not if people start laughing. I am talking about matters which touch the whole universe. I bring peace and not war. I want peace for everyone and want the earth to be full of love. The earth is disintegrating, and it is cooling down. It is still warm, but not for long, and God therefore wants love to be ever-present. People do not think of stars and therefore they cannot understand the universe. I often think of stars. I do not like astronomy, because astronomy does not explain God to us. Astronomy teaches us the geography of the stars. I do not like geography, as I dislike frontiers. To me the earth is one single state. The earth is the head of God. God is the fire in the head. I am alive as long as there is fire in my head. My pulse is like an earthquake. I know that if there are no more earthquakes the earth will get cold and all mankind with it, because people will not be able to exist.

I am spiritual food. People go to church in order to pray, and there they are made to drink wine and are told that it is the blood of Christ. The blood of Christ does not intoxicate—on the contrary it makes people sober. Catholics do not drink wine, but make use of it in a symbolic way. They swallow white wafers, thinking that they swallow the blood and flesh of our Lord. I am neither the blood nor the body of our Lord. I am the spirit in the flesh and the flesh in the spirit. There can be no God without flesh or spirit. Blood and spirit is God. I am the Lord. I am Man. I am Christ. Christ said that He was spirit in the flesh, but the church distorted His teaching, men prevented Him from living. They killed Him. He was murdered by people, who had been paid. These beggars afterwards hanged each other, because they could not live without Christ. I know that people are bad, because life is hard for them.

I want to devote myself to the theater and not films. I will leave filming to those who love to do it. I love cinematography, but I cannot devote my whole time to it. I would give up my whole life to films if people could prove that with their help one can understand one another. I know cinematography. I wanted to work in the films, but I understood their meaning. The cinema is used in order to breed money, and this is used to breed the cinema industry. I understood that the cinema brings profit only to few men, and the theater to many. The work in the theater is very hard for me, but I prefer privation to the work in the films. Diaghilev told me many a time that one should invent something on the lines of the cinema for dancing, because its force is great. Bakst, a well-known Russian painter, a Jew, said that films were good from a money point of view. I did not say anything, because I felt that Bakst and Diaghilev thought that I was but a boy and therefore kept my thoughts. Diaghilev always looks for logic in thoughts. I know that thought without logic has no value, but logic cannot exist without feeling. Diaghilev has both logic and feeling, but his feelings are bad feelings. I have good feelings. Diaghilev's head is bigger than others, but there is bad feeling in his head. Lombroso said that one can tell feelings by the shape of the head. I say that feeling can be told by the action of men. I am not a scientist, but I do understand men well. I know the tricks of the impresarios, Diaghilev is also an impresario, he has a troupe. Diaghilev has learned to cheat other impresarios. He does not like to be called an impresario, as all impresarios are supposed to be thieves. Diaghilev wants to be called "a patron of art," he wants to get into history. Diaghilev cheats people and thinks that no one sees through him. He dyes his hair in order to look young. Diaghilev's hair is white. He buys black dyes and rubs them in. I have seen this dye on Diaghilev's cushions—his pillowcase is blackened by it. I hate dirty linen and therefore was disgusted by this sight. Diaghilev has two false front teeth. When he is nervous he passes his tongue over them. Diaghilev reminds me of an angry old woman, when he moves his two false teeth. His front lock is dyed white. He wants it to be noticed. Lately this lock has grown yellow, because he has bought bad dye. In Russia it looked better. I noticed it much later, as I did not like paying attention to other people's hair. My hair bothered me too, and I was always changing its style. People said to me, "What are you doing to your hair? You always change the style." I replied that I liked changing, because I do not like to look always the same. Diaghilev liked to be talked about and therefore wore a monocle. I asked him why he wore it, for I had noticed that he could see very well without it. Diaghilev said that he could not see well with one of his eyes.

I understood that he had lied to me, and felt deeply hurt. Diaghilev was cheating me. No longer did I trust him in anything, and began to develop independently, pretending to be still his pupil. He felt my pretense and did not like me, but he knew that he was also pretending and therefore kept me. I started hating him openly and one day in the streets of Paris I pushed him in order to show him that I was not afraid of him. Diaghilev hit me with his stick as I wanted to go away from him. He felt that I wanted to leave him, and therefore ran after me. I went at a slow trot. I was afraid of being noticed. I saw people were looking. I felt pain in one leg and pushed Diaghilev, not strongly because what I felt was not anger towards Diaghilev, but sorrow. I was crying. Diaghilev was scolding me. He was grinding his teeth and I felt as depressed as if cats were scratching my soul. I could no longer control myself and started walking slowly. Diaghilev also. We walked slowly. I do not remember where we went.

After this we lived for a long, long time together. I lived sadly, and sorrowed alone. I wept alone. I loved my mother and wrote her letters every day, and wept in those letters. I spoke of my future life. I did not know what to do. I forget what I wrote exactly, but I have a feeling of having suffered bitterly. My mother felt this, because she answered my letters.

[54]

Life

She could not give a reply to my aims and ambitions, because they were my problems. She waited for my decisions. I was afraid of life because I was very young. I have now been married for over five years. I lived with Diaghilev also for five years. I cannot count. I am now about twenty-nine. I know that I was nineteen years old when I met Diaghilev. I admired him sincerely and when he told me that love for women is a terrible thing I believed him. If I had not believed him, I could not have done the things I have done. Massine does not know life, because his parents were well-off. They were short of nothing. We had no bread. Mother did not know what to give us in order to live. Mother went to the Ginizellis Circus to earn a little money. Being a well-known dancer in Russia, Mother was ashamed of such work. I understood everything as a child, and wept in my soul. My mother also cried. One day I could bear it no longer, and ran to a classmate. I ran to his father and told him that my mother was suffering, on account of lack of money. His father—a pianist—then advised me to go to the manager of the Imperial Theater. I ran there. I was only fourteen or fifteen years old. The manager was called Dmitri Ivanovich Krupensky. The director was Telikovsky. The Emperor was Nicholas II. I loved theaters. I went to the office. When I entered it, I got frightened, I saw dry, laughing faces as I entered the room where Krupensky was sitting. He had a black beard. I was afraid of him, I was afraid of the beard. I trembled like a leaf. I could not say anything to him, and was silent. Krupensky and the others started to laugh. I trembled even more; I trembled and everyone laughed. Krupensky asked me what I wanted. I told him that I needed 500 rubles to pay my mother's debts. I said this amount by chance, not thinking what I was saying. I got up. I saw bored faces. I went away. I ran quickly, panting, Krupensky and the black beard pursuing me. I ran. I silently cried: "I won't do it again, I won't do it again!" I wept in my soul, but tears would not appear. I knew that if I were to go to my mother she would understand me, therefore I ran to her and told her everything. I did not know how to lie. When I began to lie, I used to tremble like a leaf. I was a leaf of God. I loved God but I did not love praying. I did not know what to do. I lived and life passed. I did not understand business and did not like it, but God helped me. I got some dancing pupils. I was happy to earn. I often cried alone and was glad to have my separate room. I thought that I was grown up, because I had a room to myself. In a separate room I could cry a lot.

I read Dostoievsky's *The Idiot*, at the age of eighteen, and understood its meaning. I wanted to be-

come a writer and I awkwardly studied the books of
Dostoievsky and Gogol. I copied Pushkin, thinking
that if I copied I would learn to write poems and
novels like Pushkin. I copied a lot, but then felt that
this was nonsense and gave it up. I lived simply. We
had enough bread now. My mother loved entertaining people. She invited lots of people when she felt
we had enough food. She liked acquaintances and
therefore invited them. I also liked entertaining and
listened to everything the grown-ups were saying. I
understood the grown-ups and was drawn to them.
Only later I understood my mistake, because the
problems of the grown-ups were different from my
own. I loved the grown-ups because the young ones
pushed me away, they did not understand me. I knew
a boy who drank vodka. I did not drink. We were
at school together. Communal life at school united
us, but did not bring us together, because I did not
follow his habits. I do not know who had taught him
to drink so much. His face was pale and covered
with pimples. The teachers did not understand the
children; they used to lock themselves up in their
study and either read or received their friends there.
I understand teachers who feel bored in the company
of children, and I understand children who do not
understand the teachers. Education is a difficult task.
I will not have my Kyra educated in this way, know-

ing what this kind of education is. Strangers get bored
with them. People ought to educate their children
themselves, and not send them away to strangers.
The life of children depends on their education. Married teachers cannot bring up children; if they are
married they pine for their wives and family. One
teacher I knew had favorites. His name was Ivan. I
loved him, but felt he did not love me, and was afraid
of him, thinking he wished me harm. He once called
me to his flat, saying he wanted to teach me French.
I went to him, hoping that I would learn, but when
I arrived there, he made me sit on a chair and gave
me a book. I felt bored. I did not understand why he
had called me as he only gave me a book to read.

I read aloud, but remember it was boring. Ivan
asked me to eat. He paid the people with whom he
lived for board and room; they spoke Russian. The
woman was young and thin. She had bad nerves, because she moved a lot. A young man was with her, I
forget what he looked like, but remember her face
well. She had a tiny, tiny dog which kept on running
under the table, and licking her plate. She adored
that dog. I did not like him, he was ill. His body was
spoilt. It was thin; thin, long little legs; tiny ears.
Staring, small eyes. In one word, the dog was teeny-
weeny. I felt pity for the dog and grew sad. Ivan
laughed at the dog, as it was so tiny. I felt that I was

not wanted, because they wished to speak about something and kept silent about it. I felt a secret, and wanted to leave and did not know how. Ivan smiled at me. I felt disgusted and went away, leaving everything that was put on my plate. I left with a nasty feeling in my mind about Ivan and the others. I felt nauseated and could no longer go on with the French lessons, and avoided Ivan. I received bad marks for my work. I received 1. We had a system where the best mark was 12. I would not learn French, as I was disgusted. The French teacher felt this, and was angry. From now on I did not study French, and when I had to reply other pupils had to prompt me. The teacher gave me better marks. He had to show that his pupils learned well, and therefore gave me good marks. I understood his tricks and started to change the marks. I would turn a 1 into a 9. I liked changing the marks. The Frenchman did not notice anything and no one said anything to me. I gave up my French.

I did not like learning the Holy Writ, as I was very bored with it. I liked going to the Holy Writ lessons, as I liked listening to the *batiushka's**—"Little Father's"—jokes. The *batiushka*—"Little Father"—was not mine, but the father of others because he spoke

---

*A batiushka *is a Russian priest.*

of "his children." He would show us a coin and say that with that coin he taught his children to understand him. I knew my mother had no money and I understood her, therefore felt boredom. "Little Father" was not really a little father, because the "Little Father" ought to be a good man—this one was withholding his anger. All the children knew this, and therefore allowed themselves many tricks. I know boys' tricks. I often played them and the boys therefore loved me. Once I showed them that I was the best shot with a catapult I made myself; I hit the school doctor in the eye—he was sitting in a droshky —when we were all on our way to the theater in carriages. I liked carriages, because from them one could shoot at the passers-by. I aimed well. I was not sure that I hit the doctor when accused of this, but I was ashamed to deny it when all the boys pointed at me. I was frightened that the boys would all be sent away from school. I was accused of the crime and the school inspector gave me a talking-to. I was afraid of the scolding, as I felt the fury of the inspector. Porntchevsky was an angry man, but did not throw children into the street, because he knew that they were the children of poor parents. Porntchevsky called my mother and told her that he would not throw me out, but could not let me go without punishment, and therefore thought that my mother should take me home for two weeks. I felt deeply grieved and almost fainted. I was frightened for my mother, knowing how difficult it was for her to get money. My mother and I both cried. Our weeping touched the teacher, who was a very good man, but a drunkard, and all the children laughed at him, because he was funny. The children loved him, as he never hurt anyone. Many cried when we heard that he had drunk himself to death. He was buried, but not one boy went to the funeral. I was also afraid to go.

My mother gave me a good thrashing, with branches which the *dvornik** had bought. I was not afraid of a thrashing, but I was afraid of my mother. She beat me hard, but I felt no pain, because I did not feel my mother's anger. She beat me because she thought that this is the best way. I felt love for my mother and promised I would not do it again. She understood me and believed me. Feeling this, I decided to learn well. I started to get good marks and everyone laughed at me, saying that my mother's thrashing had done some good. The teachers smiled and the boys laughed. I laughed also and did not feel hurt. I loved my mother and was therefore pleased that everyone knew about it. I told them how she thrashed me. The children got frightened and no longer laughed.

*A dvornik *is a Russian porter.*

From now on I learned well and gave a good example, only the French lessons and the Holy Writ still seemed difficult. I knew the Russian Holy Writ well, as I went to church every feast day. I liked going to church, I loved the silver icons, which glittered in the sun. Candles were being sold and I sometimes sold them with Issaev, my friend. I liked him. I suffered when I felt like indulging in self-abuse. I wanted to every time that I went to bed. Ivan, my teacher, noticed that I practiced self-abuse, but did not say anything terrible to me. At school no one else knew my habits and therefore I continued until I noticed that my dances became worse. Then I got scared, understanding that my mother would soon be ruined, and I would not be able to help her. I started fighting this filthy habit—I forced myself, saying to myself: "You must not!" I learned well. I gave up self-abuse. I was about fifteen years old. I loved my mother and the love for her forced me to better myself; I learned well. Everyone started noticing my progress. I got 12 as a mark. My mother became happy and often said to me that the thrashing had done me good. I told her that that was so, but felt differently about it myself. My love for my mother was boundless. I decided to dance even more. I grew thinner and started dancing like God. Everyone started talking about it. Though still at school, I already danced

Crayon drawing done by Nijinsky while in the asylum

as the leading dancer at the theater. I knew what it
meant to be the leading dancer. I could not understand why I was given such parts to dance, but I
liked showing myself. I was proud, but did not like
praise, I did not boast.

I was liked by the pupils of the dramatic classes. I
was often with them. I met a girl pupil, who chose
me as her favorite. She called me Nijinka.* She gave
me an album bound in velvet, containing newspaper
clippings. In these clippings I read that I was called
a *Wunderkind*. The criticism was signed by Svetlov.
I disliked what they wrote about me, as I felt it was
praise. I told my school friend that I disliked all that
was written about me, but she told me that I did not
understand, and invited me to her home, saying that
she wanted me to meet her father and mother. I fell
in love with her, but did not tell her. I loved her
spiritually and therefore always smiled at her. I was
always smiling. I liked smiling at everyone, as I noticed they all loved me. I loved everyone.

When I came to my new friends, we had dinner
and then we held a seance. They put their hands on
the table and the table moved. Everyone was astonished at this. Her father, a general, disliked such
nonsense and therefore left. I also felt that this was

*Nijinka *means "tender one" in Russian.*

nonsense and left to go home. Arriving home, I was tired and could not make out for what reason I had been invited. I disliked invitations and therefore usually refused them.

I was asked to give some lessons in ballet dancing, as I had already become famous in Russia. I was sixteen. I gave lessons and earned some money. My mother pitied and felt a great love for me. I also had a great love for my mother and decided to help her with my earnings. I finished school at eighteen and graduated. I did not know how to dress—I had been used to uniforms. I did not like civil clothes and therefore did not know how to wear them. I thought that shoes with very big soles were the best-looking and therefore bought a pair with enormous soles. As I graduated I felt freedom, but this freedom frightened me. As a prize I received a Bible with an inscription, from my Holy Writ teacher. I did not understand this Bible, as it was written in Latin and in Polish. I spoke and read Polish very badly. If I had been given a Bible in Russian, I would have understood more easily. I began reading it and then gave it up. I did not like to read this Bible as it was incomprehensible to me. The book was lovely and the print beautiful. I could not feel the meaning of the Bible. I read Dostoievsky. This was easier for me and therefore I gulped it quickly down. It was a real "gulping," because when I read *The Idiot*, I felt the "idiot" was not an idiot; but a good man. I could not understand *The Idiot*, because I was too young. I did not know life. I now understand Dostoievsky's "idiot"; because I am myself being taken for an idiot. I like this feeling and therefore pretend to be an idiot. I know that nervous people can easily become mad, and was therefore afraid of madness. I am not mad, and Dostoievsky's "idiot" is *not* an idiot. I felt nervous and therefore made mistakes. God has shown me what nerves are. I do not like nervousness because I know its results. I want to write calmly and not nervously, but I do not want to write slowly, because I need not show beauty in my writing, but must write quickly. I do not want my handwriting to please. I write this book for thought and not for writing. My hand gets tired, because I am not used to writing a lot, but I know that it will soon get used to it. I feel pain in my hand and therefore write badly and dispersedly. Everyone will say that my handwriting is that of a nervous man, because the letters are scattered. My thoughts are not nervous— they flow calmly not stormily.

The thought of Wilson gives me no peace. I wish him success. I hope that my book will help him and therefore want to publish it soon. In order to publish it quickly, I want to go to Paris. But to go to

Paris, I must make preparations. I know that there are many wicked people and therefore want to protect myself. I want to write a letter to Reszké in Polish and I must get used to this language. I will tell him the whole truth and he will help me. I want to write in Polish, but not in this book. . . . I wrote a letter in Polish to Reszké.

LETTER TO JEAN DE RESZKÉ
Original in Polish

I am very sorry but I am unable to write in Polish very well, but as I am very fond of Poles I am using this language in writing to you.

I know that you are aware of my being a Pole. I do not want anything from you, only I want to ask you to kindly help me to get some documents.* At the present time it is very difficult to obtain documents, and this is why I am writing to you with a request. I ask you to find out from the French authorities if they could obtain for me the said documents.

My wife loves me and therefore she wants to be with me. I have a daughter Kyra. I gave her this name because I love Greece.† I always had a great interest for Grecian Art: it reminds me of my l'Après-midi d'un Faune.

I know that you like me, and therefore I am approaching you with my request. Although you have seen me very seldom

---

**Nijinsky is requesting a Polish passport.*
†*Kyra is an old Byzantine name.*

in my private life I know that you have friendly feelings towards me.

The reason I cannot speak Polish very well is because at the Imperial School I was not allowed to use this language. I learned the little I know from a Polish dancer; his name was Bonislavsky, he came from Warsaw. I liked Bonislavsky because, on account of his teaching, I had the opportunity to get acquainted with the works of Mickiewicz. I write also but I cannot do it as well as Mickiewicz. I know Polish literature well, through Russian translations. I know Russian much better. My mother and father left Poland in their youth. I was born in Kiev but was baptized in Warsaw in the Church of the Holy Cross. I was born in 1889. My mother had me baptized once more in Kiev; therefore my name is registered twice in the birth registers. As my mother did not want me to serve in the Russian troops of the army, she registered me in the birth register in Warsaw, hoping that through this I might be allowed to serve there.

My mother nourished me with her own milk. She was a Pole with her whole soul. . . . I was brought up in Russia as a Russian boy. Although I am a Pole as my father was, I love Russia. I dislike revolutions. I find the victory achieved by this means a horror—I consider it the victory of godless animals. I am sorry for the people, as I love them. I am myself a human being and I pity humanity. When I hear that people were killed through the revolution, I cry. I am not an anarchist, I don't belong to any party. My political views are to be kind to everybody. *I like Paderewski but I do not share his political views. I like the ideas of Wilson because I feel that he has the same intention towards all mankind. I do not want that type of politics where people quarrel and kill each other. I dislike party politics which lead to mass murder. I love everybody equally. I love my parents and I know you feel that I like you. Your wife has also several times expressed friendship towards me, I have not forgotten you all the time since we have met. . . .*

When I heard that you lost your brother I cried. I was very sorry for him, although we did not know each other personally. But I felt him and knew that you were very devoted to him.

It is very difficult for me to write fluently in Polish as I never did study this language.

I have devoted all my time to dancing, and this is why I dance well. I wish to dance in Paris and therefore I am requesting you to obtain permission for me to go to France. I have not been in contact with anybody since I came to live in Switzerland. I have occupied myself solely with dancing and with the creation of a "dance theater."

I am very fond of singing but I cannot do it. I know that you sing admirably. Although you are not any more in full possession of your voice, I am still happy to hear you sing. I am an artist in "singing through the dance." I have not lost my "voice" yet, as I am still very young. You have sung a lot in your life. The Marchioness of Ripon spoke to me very often of you, and I know how successfully you sang in

England. *You are a very famous artist—everybody admired
you and you knew everybody. I am sure, therefore, you will
be able to help me. I too have a great many admirers in Paris
but I do not know who they are. I should like to meet them,
therefore please tell all your friends that I am going to dance
at your house.*

*I have devoted a great deal of time during the war to
dancing and have made great progress. I want to show the
public how successfully I studied, but I do not want to work
any more with Diaghilev as I had a lot of unpleasantness
on account of him. I know you dislike him and you will
help me. Diaghilev thinks and says that I am "dead to art,"
but I am not "dead for art." I live today more than ever
before.*

*I am very fond of French artists and I wish I could dance
for them. I know that a lot of French artists were killed in
the war—many fathers died, leaving their children and wives
without bread. I know too that the government is unable to
provide for them all, therefore I would like to dance for the
poor French artists. I want to dance for the Polish and
other artists, too, when I go to the other countries.*

*The Poles love France because France gave them their
Soul—so did the Poles: they died for France on the battle-
fields. The war has united the two nations. France knows
the heroic deeds of the Poles. Although I do not know Polish
very well I feel the Poles. I have not written in Polish for
the last 10 years. I had nobody to write to. My father died
10 years ago in Kharkov. I always used to write to him in*

Polish. My father left my mother with us children in St. Petersburg as he wanted us to be brought up there.

The Russian Government gave us our education. Diaghilev took me to Paris. I love Paris. Paris is the heart of France. I wish I could have a place in the heart of France. . . . I hope you will be the intermediary and will obtain for me the necessary documents and help me to obtain Polish papers. The others I will get for myself. I thank you for your kindness.

À bientôt
Your loving
WASLAW NIJINSKY

He is a Pole. I paid him many compliments although I do not like compliments, as they are an unnecessary thing. I am not a man to make compliments, but a man who says the truth. The truth is different. I wrote also a letter to Diaghilev and his friends, showing them my teeth. My teeth did not bite.

LETTER TO SERGEI PAVLOVICH DIAGHILEV

To the Man,

I cannot name you because I have no name for you. I am not writing to you hastily. I don't want you to think that I am nervous, I am not. I am able to write quite calmly. And I like to do it, although I am not expressing myself in beau-

tiful sentences. *I have never studied how to do this. And what I want is to express a thought.*

I am not afraid of you, I know well that in your inner-most being you do not hate me. I love you as one loves a human being, but I do not want to work with you. But there is one thing I want you to know, that I am working a great deal. I am not dead. I am still alive. God lives in me and I live in Him. My whole time is taken up with my dancing, and my work is progressing. Whenever I can I write, too, but not beautiful sentences, which you like so much.

You are organizing troupes, I am not. I am not interested in forming companies—I am interested in human beings.

You are dead because your aims are death.

I do not call you my friend, knowing that you are my bitter enemy, but even so I have no ill feelings towards you. Enmity calls for death and I am longing for life. . . . You are malicious. I have a deep sympathy and understanding for mankind. So had Dostoievsky. He was a kind man.

You said that I am a fool and I thought that you are one. I don't want to humiliate myself before you and you love people who do that. I do not want your smile, it is death. . . . I do not smile any more, I don't bring destruction. I am not writing in order to make you merry, I am writing to make you cry.

I am a person with feeling and brains. You have brains but no feeling. Your sentiments are pernicious. You want to annihilate me and I want to save you. I love you but you don't love me. I wish you everything good, you wish me everything bad.

I know all your tricks. In the past when I was with you I often pretended to be nervous, but I was not an urchin. I was thinking deeper. I had God near me but you are a beast and do not understand love.

Don't think, don't hearken. I am not yours, you are not mine. I love you now, I loved you always. I am yours and I am my own. You have forgotten what God is, and so had I, in the past. But I found Him. You are the one who wants death and destruction, although you are afraid of death. I am not afraid of it. Death is a necessary event. We all have to die, therefore I am always prepared for it. I love love, but I am not the flesh and blood, I am the spirit, the soul. I am love. . . . You did not want to understand me to live with me in true friendship. I wish you everything good.

I want to explain to you a great deal, but I never again want to work with you, as you have utterly different aims. You are a hypocrite, and I don't want to become one. I can only admit hypocrisy when a man wants to achieve something good and noble through this means.

You are a bad man, you are not a Tsar, a ruler. You are not my Emperor. You are an evil person. You wish me harm, but I do not want this for you. I am a tender being and want to write you a cradle song . . . a lullaby. . . .*

Sleep peacefully, sleep, sleep peacefully.

Man to Man,

VASLAV NIJINSKY

*The Lullaby is written in verse and its translation is not possible.

Life

I do not like eating meat because I have seen lambs and pigs killed. I saw and felt their pain. They felt the approaching death, I left in order not to see their death. I could not bear it. I cried like a child. I ran up a hill and could not breathe. I felt that I was choking. I felt the death of the lamb. I chose a mountain, where there were no people. I was afraid of being ridiculed. Men do not understand each other. I understand men, and wish them no harm. I want to save them from evil. They do not want to be saved and therefore I do not want to be a nuisance. Being a nuisance will not save them. I want to be saved too. My star says to me: "Come here, come here!" I know what its twinkling means, knowing what life is. Life is life and not death. I cannot write because I am tired, tired because I slept, slept, and slept. I want to write now. I will go to sleep when God orders me to. I am to listen. I am in God. God, God, God. I wrote to everyone in France in French, except Reszké. He has many connections. I will therefore ask him to send me Polish papers. By this I mean my birth certificate and christening certificate. I was christened in two towns. I was born in Kiev, which is my home town. My mother cannot say anything now. I beg for her love. I want her love.

I want to describe my walks. I liked going for walks alone. I love being alone. We are all alone. We are rhythm. We are, we are you and they. I want to say, say, that thou wantest to sleep. I want to write and sleep. I write, write, write. I want to tell you that one mustn't. I want to tell you that one can't. I want to write, write. I wrote in the same manner in French and hope that I will be understood. I want to tell people about love for each other. I know that they will laugh when they receive these letters, but they will be astonished at these poems. I know that everyone thinks that I am dead, because I have not let anybody hear from me. I want to be forgotten now in order to create a strong impression later. My first appearance will be in Paris, at the Châtelet. I like this theater, because it is large and simple. I don't want much money for myself, as I want to give a performance for the poor French actors who suffered from the war. I want to make them understand about love for each other, and want to speak to them. I want them to come to me. I know that they will come to me after this "charity performance." I want to talk to all the artists, because I want to help them. I will tell them how I love them and that I will always help them. I shall often come and see them, if they will love one another. I will pretend to be a clown, because then they will understand me better. I love Shakespeare's clowns—they have a lot of humor, but nevertheless they express hate, they are not from God. I am a clown of God, and therefore like joking. I mean that a clown is all right when he expresses love. A clown without love is not from God. I feel the cold in my feet and understand that I must soon go to bed. They are walking upstairs and I feel that they will come to fetch me, but do not want to go to sleep, as I slept a lot during the daytime, but they want me to.

To my dear, beloved Romuska.

I angered you purposely, because I love you, and wish you happiness. You are frightened of me, because I changed. I did this because God so willed. God wished it, and I wished it too. You called a doctor. You believed a stranger and not me. You think that he agrees with me. But he is afraid to show that he knows nothing. Nothing, because everything he learned about the soul and brain was nothing. I was not afraid to put aside all teachings and to show everyone that I knew nothing. I can no longer dance as before, as all dances are death. By death I do not mean only the state of things when the body dies. The body dies, but the soul lives. The soul is a dove, in God. I am in God. You are a woman like all others. I am a man like all others, but I work more than the others. I know more than all the others. You will understand me later, because everyone will say that Nijinsky is like God. You will believe it.

I want often to walk with you, but you do not want

it. You think that I am ill, because the doctor told you that I was. He thinks that I am ill. I am writing to you in my book, because I want you to read it in Russian. I have learned to speak French. Do you not want to speak Russian? I wept with joy when I heard your Russian speech. You do not like me to learn Hungarian? I love the Hungarian language because you are Hungarian. I want to live in Russia. You do not know what you want. I know what I want. I want to build a house in the country. You do not want to live there. I wish you no evil, I love you. You do not want to show that you do love me. Love me! Love me! I want to tell you that you love me. Admit love. . . .

I was called to lunch at half-past twelve. I wanted to eat. I did not lunch as I saw meat. My wife wanted to eat it. I left the soup, which was made out of meat, my wife became angry. She thought that I disliked the food. I dislike meat, because I know how the animals are killed and how they cry. I wanted to show her that marriage is nonexistent if people are of different opinion. I threw the wedding ring on the table, then took it and put it on again. My wife was terribly nervous. I threw the ring once more, because I felt that she was wanting meat. I love animals and could not therefore eat their flesh, knowing that if I did, another animal would have to be killed. I only

[76]

eat when I am hungry. My wife is sorry for me and
thinks that I must eat. I like bread and butter and
cheese and eggs. I eat very little for my constitution,
and I feel better since I have not eaten meat. I know
that doctors will say that all this is nonsense—that
meat is necessary. But it is not; it arouses lecherous
feelings. Those feelings have disappeared since I have
not eaten meat. I know that children who eat meat
often practice self-abuse. Men and women separately
and together practice self-abuse too. This develops
idiocy. Man loses all sense and feeling. I used to lose
sense too when I practiced self-abuse, and trembled
as if I had fever, and had a headache. I was ill. I
know that Gogol used to do the same, and masturba-
tion was his downfall. Gogol was a sensitive man. I
know how he felt, his feeling became dumber and
dumber day by day. He felt his death approaching,
and tore up his last works. I will not destroy my
work.

Kyra is still little. I often tell her that she must not
lie on her stomach, when sleeping. When I sleep I do
so, but my stomach is small and therefore can bear
it. People who have large stomachs must not lie on
them. Men should sleep on the side and women on
the back. I learned all this as I noticed a great tiredness. I get up lazily and have no wish to live. Since I
gave up meat I feel better. My thoughts are clearer

and I run instead of walking. I only walk for a rest. I run a lot because I feel a force in me; my muscles, my hair, are more obedient. I dance more lightly, and I have a big appetite. I eat quickly. Food is not important for me, as I make nothing of it and eat what comes along, except tinned food. I am a vegetarian. I am a man and not a beast. My wife feels that one should not eat meat, but she is afraid to give it up. She thinks that doctors know more about it than I. Doctors and specialists like to eat a lot, thinking that food gives strength, but I think that force comes not from food but from the mind. People think one cannot be fed by the mind. One can; mind replaces food. I eat only as much as the mind tells me.

I ran away from home as my wife did not understand me. She got frightened of me and I got frightened of her. I did not want her to eat. She thought that I wanted to make her die of hunger. I want to help her and therefore did not want her to eat meat. I ran away from home. I ran and ran down the hill on which the house stood. Ran and ran. I did not stumble. An unseen force was pushing me forward. I was not angry with my wife. I was calm. At the bottom of the hill was the village of St. Moritz. I later turned down a road which leads to the lake. I walked quickly. Walking through the town, I saw the doctor. I walked quickly, bowing my head as if I

were at fault. When I came to the level of the lake I
started looking for a hiding-place. I had 1 franc and
10 centimes in my pocket, and remembered that I
had still a few hundred francs in the bank. I realized
that I could pay for a room and decided not to return home and to look for a lodging. I walked into a
pastry shop* to ask the owner of the shop and of the
house to let me have a room there. Wanting to melt
her heart, I told her that I had not eaten anything,
but first asked if she had. She said that she had finished lunch. I told her I was hungry. She did not say
anything to that, probably thinking that I should not
eat. In the past I had often been in that shop and
bought sweets there; she thought that I was rich and
was therefore always very pleasant to me. I kissed
her child and patted it on the head; she was pleased.
I told her that I was sorry for her, because she had
suffered on account of the war. She complained of
the hard times, I pitied her and ordered many sweets,
thinking of helping her. I asked if she could let a
room. She said that her house was all occupied. After
a time she promised that there would be a flat avail-
able in a week. I explained that I did not want a flat.
She answered that she was sorry for me, but could
not let me have a room. She thought that I wanted

Hanselmann's pastry shop in the village of St. Moritz.

to bring a woman there. I told her openly that I wanted one room to work in, as my wife did not understand me. She listened to my complaint and went out. Her husband who was present at the conversation knew that I was a serious man and needed no women—he understood me but could do nothing. I said to him that in marriage sometimes it is difficult to understand each other. He answered that once his wife picked up a plate in a wrong way and he advised her to pick it up in another way, but she did not listen to him. I understood the husband's complaint. I shook his hand for the first time and left. I was sad, because I understood that I would have to sleep in the street. I walked. I passed a row of shops. They were shut, so was the whole of Bad St. Moritz.* No one lived there. I sat down by a wall underneath a window to see if I could sleep there or not. After a while, I felt warmer, then cold. I saw a woman leaving a house, she was trembling with cold, so was I. It was bitterly cold; it was winter—at an altitude of 2,000 meters. I walked on, I suddenly saw an open door and entered. There was no one there, and I walked through the rooms. Noticing a half-open door I suddenly smelt an unpleasant odor. It came from within. I looked in and saw a dirty lavatory. I al-

---

*Bad St. Moritz is closed in the winter.

most wept at the thought of having to sleep in this dirty place. I walked into the street, which was empty. I walked on, I suddenly felt I had to move to the left. Before I walked along on the wrong street. At a distance I saw a small whitewashed house, I walked towards it, and entered. The owner was by no means a simple woman. She was dressed in town clothes. I asked her if she could let me have a room, she said she could, but that the room was not heated. I told her that I did not mind. She beckoned me to the second floor. The stairs were high, the steps were broken and outside the house. The stairs did not creak, but the snow did. I entered in room no. 5 and saw its poorness, and felt relieved. I asked how much I had to pay for it. She answered 1 franc per day. The house was white and clean. One could see that the people were poor but neat. I wanted to leave, but could not, I wanted to write in that room as I liked it. I looked around and saw a hard bed without cushions and armchairs in a row. Near the bed stood a washstand of old wood with no basin or jug. I wanted to stay; but God told me to go. Thanking her I went away, promising to come back in the evening. We parted. The woman had made a good impression on me. I walked on the same road by which I had come. I felt sadness, which was deeply rooted. From the little house I saw my own home and wept. I was

deeply unhappy and wanted to sob, but my grief
was too deep. The tears would not fall. I was saddened for a long time. I walked through a wood, and
entered another house on the way. I saw some children. They thought that I wanted to play with them;
they started to throw snowballs at me. I began to
throw smaller snowballs at them, saying, "That is
not nice." I could speak no German, but understood
the children; then taking a sled I started giving them
a ride. They laughed. I was happy. I went into the
cottage with them and saw a woman. She gave the
children sugared cookies. I wanted some as I had
not eaten anything. She understood me and gave me
a cookie. I wanted to give her 10 centimes for it, but
she wouldn't take it. Pushing it into her hand, I said
that it was for the poor children. She told me her
sorrows, that she had lost a child three months ago,
and pointed to the cemetery. I said to her I understood her grief and told her not to sorrow, because
God had taken her child, as it was God's wish. She
grew silent; she felt that this was the truth. I told her
that God takes what He gives and one should not
grieve. She grew calmer and began to smile. I wanted
to go away, but she gave another cookie to each of
the children, and I stood there. She gave me another
cookie too. She did not eat herself. She understood
me. I thanked her and left. The children loved me

although I played with them not more than a quarter of an hour. I went by the road into the wood.
There I heard the birds and sometimes the voices of
men who were skiing. I had no skis, but did not fall.*
In spite of this I walked and walked. I did not fall
because I followed the footpath. I could not walk
further, because my feet were cold. I was dressed
lightly. Walking quickly uphill, I stopped suddenly
and did not know what to do. I waited for God's
orders, waited and waited. I felt cold. I felt warm. I
knew that before freezing to death people feel cold,
but I was not afraid of dying or freezing. Then I felt
a push and went forward, went higher, walked and
walked, suddenly stopped and understood that one
could go no farther. I stopped and felt cold, felt that
death had come. I was not afraid and thought that
I would lie down; later I would be picked up and
brought to my wife. I wept in my soul and felt bitterly sad. I did not know what to do or where to go,
knowing that if I were to walk further, I could only
find a shelter about 25 versts† away. I was afraid of
freezing and was tired. I turned and walked back
along that path and saw people. I felt suddenly happy.
They took no notice of me. I walked on, admiring

* *The mountains and woods are under snow in the winter—sometimes
five to six feet high; therefore walking without skis is not possible.*
† *A verst is 3500 feet.*

them on the skis. I was walking on a rotten path full
of holes. I could not look down on the side of the
road where, at the bottom of the precipice, the Inn
was flowing. The Inn springs from where I walked.
I was tired and walked and walked. I wanted rest.
I saw a tree stump, but it was on the edge of the
road which led to a tavern. I tried to sit down, but almost fell into the stream, which was running quickly,
because the mountain was high. I walked and walked.
I felt a great tiredness, but suddenly sensed a force in
me and wanted to run the whole 25 versts, not understanding the distance. I hoped I could cover the
distance quickly by running, but felt tiredness. I
walked and walked, and wanted to run into the road
by which I came, but felt cold and decided to walk
on. I went into the village of Campfer. Here I heard
children singing. But their singing did not come from
the heart. They were songs taught to them, so I passed.
I was sorry for the children, understanding what
schools are. I walked and walked, and came to a
road which led home one way, and to my new room
the other way. I felt that I should walk to my new
room in order to change my whole life, and decided
to go there, but an unknown power forced me to realize that I had to turn to my house. The road was
long, uphill. I walked and walked, suddenly felt tired,
and sat down at the edge of the road. I sat and

rested. I felt cold, freezing, but was afraid of death. I still felt a lot of warmth in me. I sat and rested. I saw passing sleighs, passers-by, but I did not move. I thought that I would have to sit endlessly, but suddenly felt enough strength to get up. I got up and walked. I saw carts with timber and went along by their side. I saw a horse running uphill and ran myself. I was doing this without thinking, only feeling. I ran and panted, then could not run any more, and walked. I understood that men urge horses and people on, till they fall down like stones, exhausted. I decided, like the horse, that they could beat us with a whip as much as they liked, but we would still do what we feel, because we want to live. The horse walked and so did I. In the sleigh a fat man was sitting with his wife, who was bored. So was the driver. Everyone was bored. I was not, because I was not thinking, I was feeling. I walked and walked, I came to the village of St. Moritz and stopped outside the telegraph office. I did not read the war bulletins. Suddenly someone grabbed hold of me by the shoulder. I turned and saw the doctor. He wanted me to go to their house, but I refused point-blank, saying that I could talk to no one today as I wanted to be alone. He said that it would be better if I were to go to them, as my wife was there too. I told him that I hated peacemaking. I liked people to understand each other and not just make up quarrels. I liked this doctor. I felt that he was bitterly sad. I was also unhappy, but decided to go home, my *own* home, and walked towards it quickly. I walked up the hill and before reaching the house I saw the doors open. Louise, the servant, was opening the doors for me. I entered and sat down at the piano and started playing; I played a funeral march. My soul cried. The servant felt all and said: "It is beautiful."

I finished playing and went to eat. She gave me all sorts of things. I ate bread and butter with cheese, and as dessert two jam pastries. I was not really hungry. I came to write all this. Later I was called for dinner, but I refused point-blank, as I did not want to eat alone, saying I was not a child to be coaxed. Louise was coaxing me by saying, "Hot spaghetti." I did not answer anything.

They are ringing and ringing. I do not know who is calling as I do not like speaking on the telephone. It must be my wife's mother, she has arrived and is ringing up to inquire after my health. The servant with tears in her voice is answering something. Everyone thinks that I am ill. I am writing, crying, and thinking of my wife, who went out thinking that I am a barbarian of Russian origin. She heard these words in Hungary, when Russia was at war with Hungary. I was interned there. I lived there and composed the *Theory of the Dance*. I danced very little because I was sad, sad because I thought that my wife did not love me. I got engaged in Rio de Janeiro; I married suddenly in South America. I met her on the steamer *Avon*. I have already described my married life a little. I must say that I married without thinking of the future. We spent money, which I had saved with great difficulty. I gave her roses at 5 francs each. I brought her twenty to thirty of these roses a day. I liked giving them to her, as I felt flowers and understood that my love is white, not red. Red roses frighten me. I am no coward. I married. I felt everlasting love and not a sensual love. I loved her passionately and gave her all I could. She loved me. It seemed to me that she was happy. For the first time I felt grieved three or five days after my wedding. I asked my wife to learn to dance, because dancing was the highest thing in life for me. I wanted to teach her. I never taught anyone my art, I wanted it for myself, but I wanted to teach her the real art of the dance, but she got frightened. Did she no longer trust me? I wept and wept bitterly, and already felt death. I understood that I had made a mistake, but it was too late to undo it. Had I put myself into the arms of a person who did not love me? I understood the whole mistake. My wife worshiped me above all, but she did not feel me. I wanted to leave, but understood that that would be caddish, and stayed with her. She loved me. Did she love me for my art and for the beauty of my body?

She was clever and taught me about the necessary things of life. I had a lawsuit in London against the Palace Theater and lost it. I still have a lawsuit against that theater. I have already described that management. I collapsed from overwork and had an attack of fever and was at death's door. My wife cried then. She loved me and suffered when she saw that I overworked myself. She understood that it was on account of money. I did not want money, but only a simple life. I loved the theater and wanted to work. I worked hard, but later my spirits fell as I noticed that I was not liked, and I retired into myself. I retired so far that I could no longer understand people. I wept and wept.

I do not know why my wife cries. I think that she has realized now the mistake and is afraid that I will leave her. I did not know that she was with my daughter at home. I thought that they were out. I stopped as I heard weeping. I am hurt deeply and am sorry for her. I weep, weep. She weeps and weeps. Friends are with her and therefore I will not go to her. I hope that God will help and that she will understand.

LETTER TO LADY "X"

Dear Madam,

I was very happy to receive your letter—I understood your intention to let me know that the performances of the Russian Ballet are not as good as they used to be. Also, I felt that you wished to let me know that Massine is speaking well of me. I believe that he does speak kindly, but I feel at the same time that this is a pretense. I believe this to be so because Massine has a great affection for Diaghilev, whom I dislike.

Diaghilev hates me: he tried to put me in prison in Barcelona. I danced in Barcelona—as I always do—with "love." Massine dances without love, as he prefers the dramatic art. He is a good boy—I have a real affection for him, but I do not think that he has friendly feelings towards me, as he thinks I hurt Diaghilev. Diaghilev told him that the reason he dislikes me is because I asked for the salary I was to have received in his company.

Diaghilev dislikes to pay—Massine will find this out in time. I wish to be paid punctually—I have a mother who would starve if I did not look after her. Massine likes the money as well as I do. I do not mind if Massine has taken my place in your heart. I like him, and I kissed him like a brother when we met—but he did not return my kiss and this made me sad——

I do not want to work any more with Diaghilev—in the future I will work always without him as our ideas are utterly different. I hope that Massine—whom I appreciate—will come to me. I hope he will not be frightened by Diaghilev and that he will allow Massine to join me.

One time I was frightened, too, by Diaghilev but not any more—I am working very hard and am making great progress. But this progress is very different from that Diaghilev makes. I am different from Diaghilev, I have a heart—and I work with my heart and soul and hope to develop my spirit. I am no longer Nijinsky of the Russian Ballet—I am Nijinsky of God—I love Him and God loves me——

I want you to see my dances now—without a company. For this reason I want you to come and see me in Paris, where I intend to go soon.

> *Hoping to see you soon,*
> *With friendship,*
> *Yours,*
> VASLAV NIJINSKY

TO THE MARCHIONESS OF RIPON, 1919

Dear Madam,

I want to ask you to forward the enclosed letter to Dmitri Romanovich Kostrowsky. He is an artist and he suffers from epilepsy, but he is very intelligent.

I have a great affection for him and for this reason I am writing to him. I leave this letter open—I have no secrets. Would you please forward this letter in your name, as I do not want it to go astray? Will you show this letter if neces-

sary to the English authorities; also I want to beg you to
allow Kostrowsky to write to me care of you.

I have another great favor to ask you to protect Kostrowsky, as he is very ill—and very poor—he is with his wife.
His children are in Russia and I believe his wife is suffering, because she could not see the children. I do not want
Kostrowsky to leave for Russia; it would be better if Madame
Kostrowsky would go alone to Russia. I understand they are
afraid of the Bolsheviks. My mother went to Kiev, as she
was afraid to during the Revolution.

I am sure the authorities will understand why I ask permission for Madame Kostrowsky to leave for Russia.

I thank you in advance,

With friendship,

WASLAW NIJINSKY

TO THE PRESIDENT OF THE COUNCIL
OF THE ALLIED FORCES IN RUSSIA, PARIS

Your Excellency,

I want to ask you to allow the enclosed letter to be deliv-
ered to my mother. I love my mother and I want her to know
that I am alive. I know that you are frightfully busy, but I
know also that you are a kind man.

You will understand me if you have seen me dance.

I beg you to do me the favor and to forward my letter to
my mother. I know it depends of you, although you have to
submit it to the other authorities.

Once more I ask you to forward it. My mother is a sick

woman. She has lost a son and she suffers because she cannot see me. She loves me. She has nothing to do with politics and is 70 years old. She knows that I am famous and loved everywhere, that I have influential friends and therefore, if she does not hear of me, she will believe that I am dead.

It is over a year and a half since I have been able to communicate with her. She might think that I danced lately in England. Probably she will be frightened lest I be harmed on account of the revolution, as they might think I belong to the revolutionaries. My mother knows I do not belong to any political creed or party. She knows of my love towards mankind. She knows I dislike forcefulness. She knows that even when I was a boy I disliked to fight with my classmates. She brought me up, she knows me well. I dislike fights—I love everybody—and do not want the death of anybody.

I love my wife. She is Hungarian born. I traveled with her during the war, in France. The French authorities permitted us to go through France, several times. I love France and England, Poland, Italy, and Russia. I love the whole world.

I thank you in advance,
WASLAW NIJINSKY

Life

The letter begins in Russian, but ends in Polish. Nijinsky's
mother lived in Russia.

My dear Mother,

*I love you as always and I am in good health. I have had
no news from you. I have written to you but have not received any reply and my letters were returned to me.*

*I am happy. But I am unhappy because I cannot see you.
I love you and ask you to come to me. I have a little house
which I have rented furnished; this house is at your disposal.
I love you so much, you have brought me up. I have a daughter, and I wish you would bring her up, too. I know how
much of God you have in yourself, therefore I wish you to
give Him to my daughter. My daughter is a marvelous child.
She listens to those who love her, therefore she will obey you.
God wishes that you should be with her and I want you to
be with me. Come immediately. I will send you money for
the journey. I don't want to be mixed up in politics. I am
not a politician, I am a human being, creation of God. I
love everybody and don't approve of any kind of murder. I
am young, strong, and I work a great deal. I have not much
money but sufficient to provide for you all your life.*

I want to see Bronia and Sacha too. They are now
with you. I know they are devoted to you. I realize that they
have a very hard time to earn their living and are tired of*

**Bronia is Nijinsky's sister, Sacha his brother-in-law.*

[93]

struggling. I wish to help them. I do not want money for myself.

My wife loves you too and wants you to come very much. So do I. Write to me, please, through the British authorities. I am sending this letter also through them. I know they will like you if you go to present yourself. But go alone, without Sacha. They might disapprove of the revolutionaries. I don't know how Sacha is now, as I have not seen him for a long time.

I liked Kerensky but disapproved of the Maximalists. Now I do not know how he is as he does not express himself lately. I do express my opinions. I dislike party politics. I don't belong to any party. I know too well that God loves all people and does not wish anybody's death.

Many people misunderstood Tolstoy. He was not an Anarchist. I read his works many times. I see that he loved everybody. He loved God and not a party. I also do the same. My party is God's party; he is with me, I am with Him.

I kiss you, my dear mother, and ask you to kiss all those who love me.

Your son
WACIO

Pencil drawings done by Nijinsky

Книга вторая.

О смерти

В. Нижинскій

Сантъ-Морицъ-Дорфъ.

Вилла Гуадалупъ

27 февраля 1919 года.

Facsimile of Book II of Death

PART TWO

DEATH

*February 27, 1919**

ABOUT DEATH.

DEATH CAME UNEXPECTEDLY—for I wanted it to come.
I told myself I did not wish to live. I did not live
long. I was told I was mad. I thought I was alive,
but wasn't given any peace. I lived and was glad but
people said that I was wicked. I decided to write
about death. I cry and am very grieved, for everything around me is empty. Louise, the maid, will cry
tomorrow, for she will be sad, seeing all this destruction and waste. I have taken down all the pictures
and drawings at which I had been working for six
months. My wife will look for these pictures and will
not find them. I have moved the furniture back to its
old place and put the old lampshade where it was
before. I do not want people to laugh at me and have
decided not to do anything. God tells me not to do
anything else, only to write down my impressions. I
will write. I want to understand my wife's mother

* *This is the only date Nijinsky placed in the manuscript of his diary.
It is the last entry and indicates the end of his manuscript.*

and her husband. I know them well, but I want to be sure.

I write about the things I have lived through and am not imagining anything. I am sitting at an empty table. In the drawer are all my paints. They have dried up, for I do not do any more painting. I have done a lot and made good progress. I want to paint but not here, as I feel death. I want to go to Paris, but I am afraid I will be too late. I want to write now about death. I will call the first part of this book "Life," and this part "Death." I will make people understand life and death and I hope to be successful. I know that if I publish these books people will say that I am a bad writer, but I do not want to be a writer. I want to be a thinker. Mind is life, not death. I write about philosophy but I am not a philosopher. I do not like philosophy because it is a whim of spoiled people. I am not Schopenhauer. I am Nijinsky. I am the one who dies when he is not loved. I pity myself as I pity God. God loves me and will give me life in death. I do not want to sleep. I am writing at night. My wife is not asleep either, she is thinking. I feel death.

I understand people. They want to enjoy life, loving the pleasures of life. All pleasures are horrible. I do not want pleasure. My wife will be frightened when she finds out that everything I write is the truth. I know she will be sad because she will think that I do not love her. It is possible she will not want to live with me any more, because she will not trust me. I love her and I will suffer without her. But my sufferings are necessary and I will bear them. I cannot hide the things I know. I must show the meaning of life and death. I want to describe death. I love it —I know what it is. Death is horrible. I have felt death many times.

I was dying in a hospital when I was fifteen years old. I was a brave boy. I had been jumping and fell. They took me to a hospital. There I saw death with my own eyes. I saw a patient foaming at the mouth. It was because he drank a whole bottle of medicine, which keeps one well, but if one drinks it all it makes one die and leave this world. Beyond this world there is no light, and therefore I am afraid of death and what is beyond. I want light, the light of twinkling stars. A twinkling star is life—and a star that does not twinkle is death. I have noticed there are many human beings who do not twinkle. Death is an extinguished life. The life of people who have lost their reason is an extinguished life. I have also been mad. I had lost my reason, but I understood the truth when I was left in St. Moritz—for I have felt deeply about things. I know it is difficult to feel when one is alone. But only alone can one understand feeling.

I know it is my fault that my wife is trying to calculate. I have told her not to do it, for all accounts have been settled. I want to go and have a drink and to eat and, after, to write down my impressions. I will write about all the things I see and hear.

I drank the whole bottle of mineral water. I want to live as I have lived before. After finishing this book I will do so. I want to write about death and therefore I must have impressions fresh in my mind. When a man writes about his experiences, this must be so. I will write about all my experiences I want to live through.

I know that everyone will be frightened of me and they will put me into a lunatic asylum, but I do not care. I am not afraid of anything, and want to die. I will be ready for everything. God wishes to improve life and I will be His instrument.

It is past one o'clock and I am still awake. People ought to work during the day but I work at night; tomorrow my eyes will be red. My mother-in-law will be frightened and will think that I am mad. I hope I will be sent to an asylum. Once I created a ballet to the music of Richard Strauss. I composed this ballet in New York and produced it quickly. I was asked to do it in three weeks. I protested, saying that I could not produce a ballet in three weeks and that it was not in my power to do it so quickly. Otto Kahn, the di-

rector of the Metropolitan Opera, said that he could
not give me longer. He informed me through Mr.
Coppicus, who was sent to negotiate with me about
the affairs of the theater. I agreed to this proposal—
for I could do nothing else, knowing that if I refused
I would have no money to live on. I decided and went
to work. I worked like an ox. I was tireless and slept
very little. I worked and worked. My wife saw all this
work and felt sorry for me. I engaged a masseur—
without massage I could not have gone on with my
work. I realized that I was almost dying. I ordered
the costumes in America from a *costumier*. I explained
to him all the details. He understood my ideas. I commissioned an American, Robert Edmond Jones, to do
the sets. This artist, although he tried to understand
me, did not seem to have the right feeling for the
scenery. He worried and worried the whole time. I
did not worry, but explained to him the *décors* I
wanted, and I told him to bring books of the period
which had to be represented. He drew as I explained
to him. The drawings of the costumes were better.
Their colors were full of life. I love life full of color.
He understood when I showed him how to find the
right idea and was grateful, but he still worried and
worried. He reminds me of my wife who is afraid of
everything. I used to say to him, "Why should you be
afraid? One must not be afraid." But he still worried.

Evidently he worried about the success of the ballet. He did not believe in me. I was certain of success. I worked like an ox, but the ox was driven too hard—he fell and twisted his foot.

I was taken to Dr. Abbé, a good doctor. His cure was simple. He ordered me to lie down and rest. I stayed in bed and rested. I had a nurse. She sat by me the whole time. I could not sleep because I was not used to sleeping with a nurse watching me in the room. If she had been sleeping instead of sitting there staring at me, I would have been able to sleep. She kept on saying all the time, "Do try and sleep, do sleep." But I could not. Two weeks passed like this. My ballet *Till** was not yet produced. The public became restless, thinking I was a capricious artist. I was not afraid of the public's opinion. The directors decided to put off this ballet for a week. In the meantime they started the season without me, hoping to do business as they were afraid of financial failure, but there was no failure because as soon as I started to dance the public came.

The American public loves me—they believe in me. They saw that my foot was hurting. I danced badly, but they were glad. *Till* had a great success, but it was produced too quickly. It was "taken out of the

---

* *The ballet to which Nijinsky refers is* TILL EULENSPIEGEL, *first produced in America in 1916.*

oven" too soon, and therefore was raw. The American public liked my "raw" ballet. It tasted good, as I cooked it very well. I did not like this ballet but said, "It is good." One had to say it, otherwise no one would have come to the theater and the season would have been a financial failure. I do not like failure and therefore said, "It is good." I told Otto Kahn that I was happy about it and pleased. He complimented me as he saw how pleased the public was. I made it a comic ballet, as I was sensitive and felt the war. Everyone was fed up with the war. People had to be cheered up. I cheered them up. I showed them *Till* in all its beauty, a simple beauty. I showed them the real German people. The papers were pleased because the critics were mostly German. Before the first performance I called the journalists and explained to them the object and story of *Till*. They were extremely pleased because they could prepare their reviews. The criticisms were very good and some of them very intelligent. I was raised to great heights. I did not like these because I felt it was nothing but praise. I do not like praise because I am not a boy. The critics understood my ballet. I saw the fault which had been noticed by one of the critics. He noticed a particular bit in the music which he thought I did not understand. I understood very well, but I did not want to tire myself, as my foot was still hurting. This particular bit was very difficult for the performer, therefore I did not bother about it. The critics always think that they are cleverer than the artists. They often abuse their rights when they scold the artist for his performance. Artists are poor and tremble before the critic. They feel hurt and suffer. The soul weeps.

I know of an artist and a critic whose name is Alexandre Benois. He is an intelligent man and has a great knowledge of paintings. I read his criticisms *Letters on Art*. He was always attacking Alexandre Golovin who was the scenic painter at the Imperial Theater in St. Petersburg. He sent his criticism to the newspaper *Retch*.* This paper was directed by Nabokov, who was an intelligent man. He asked Filosovov to join him. He wrote always against the paper *Novoë Vremia*. *Retch* was trying to get hold of the subscribers of *Novoë Vremia*, but *Retch* was an empty, stupid paper.

I already understood newspapers and journalism when I was a boy. They wrote about hackneyed things which one knew without having to read about them. They filled pages because the pages had to be filled. I was not afraid of criticism when I was a boy and therefore did not bow to the critics. I bowed to

*Retch *means speech, in Russian.*

one whose name was Valerian Svetlov. He was a
critic on dancing. He lived with a dancer and learned
many technical expressions about dancing from her.
He made them up into beautiful sentences. There
were other critics on dancing but they were not so
sharp and witty. Svetlov was always ready with an
answer. He took a lot of trouble with his criticisms
and wrote well. People thought that a man who writes
well would understand the art of dancing, but this
is not the case. I understood the art of dancing because I danced. Svetlov had never danced in any of
the ballets he wrote about, and did not know what
dancing means. He was called the Parrot because he
looked like a parrot. Nikolai Legat* did not like him
and drew caricatures of him, looking like a parrot. I
call him a parrot not because his head looks like it,
but because in his writings he repeats things like all
those critics who repeat things that are already well-
known. Svetlov was dressed in silk. He smelt of per-
fume and face creams. He had money. He gave his
friend expensive presents. He didn't make love to
her as a young man would. He was nearly sixty years
old and used to make up his face. Women liked him.
His criticisms were witty and to the point. Everybody was afraid of him. All the women dancers gave

*Nikolai Legat, one of Nijinsky's dancing masters at the Imperial
School.

in to him because they feared him. Life was easy for
him and he was always pleased. The expression of
his face was always quiet, like a mask. I have seen
such masks, made of wax. I believe he did not smile
because he was afraid of getting wrinkles. He owned
cuttings from old newspapers about the ballets and
always wrote the same things, just changed the style
a little. His criticisms did not convey anything new.
Just because he fancied it, he started criticizing me.
He did not know that his criticisms made me feel
sick. I was afraid of him and did not like him. I knew
that his criticisms were widely read and therefore
it was most unpleasant—for I thought I would be
forced, on account of this, to dance in the *corps de
ballet*—a crowd ignorant of art. I know many dancers who danced very well; they studied tremendously,
but were put in the *corps de ballet* for lack of protec-
tion and influence. The *corps de ballet* was quite good,
because there were some clever dancers in it. They
liked me and this was a good advertisement for me.
Already in those days I wanted people to like and to
love me. Not only did I want the *corps de ballet* to
love me—but also the first and second dancers, the
ballet masters and ballerinas, too. I sought love and
realized there was none. It was all filth. Everyone
wanted praise and flattery. I did not like flattery and
praise.

[106]

Death

I used to go to the office of the intendant of the theaters, Krupensky, and asked him to be allowed to dance. I only danced four times a year. A ballet season is eight months a year. I danced very rarely in St. Petersburg in front of the public, although the public was very fond of me. I knew this was the result of the intrigues of other dancers. I was no longer gay, I felt death, and was afraid of people and locked myself up in my room. I had a narrow room with a high ceiling. I liked looking at the walls and ceiling because it made me think of death. I did not know how to cheer myself up.

I do not think one should preserve pictures of dead painters because they harm young painters. A new young artist is compared always with the Old Masters. A painter was not graduated from the Academy of Painting only because his pictures did not resemble the pictures in museums. This painter was called Anisfeld, a Jew. He is married and has children. He quarreled with his wife. I remember. He used to come to Diaghilev and complain about it. I know that he loved his wife, I felt his soul was crying. He was a good man. I commissioned scenery for several ballets from him. Now he paints portraits and *décors* in North America. One sees in the papers that he is successful. Bakst was angry with Anisfeld. He did not like Anisfeld because he painted good *décors* and had a great success in Paris and other towns where we performed.

Our company called itself the Russian Ballet. I loved the Russian Ballet. I gave my heart and soul to it. I worked like an ox and I lived like a martyr. I knew how hard it was for Diaghilev too. I realized his difficulties. He suffered on account of money. He did not love me when I did not give him all my earnings which he used for the ballets. All my savings. Diaghilev once asked me for 40,000 francs. I gave them to him but I was afraid that he would not return the money. I knew he had not got it. I realized that Diaghilev knew how to find money and therefore decided to refuse if he asked me again. Diaghilev again asked me behind the scenes at the Châtelet in Paris—as he happened to be passing. I quickly told him that I did not want to give him my salary any more. I wanted this money for my mother. I did not want her to suffer on account of money. My mother had suffered a lot in the past, I wanted her to have a peaceful life now. I noticed that she was worried about me. She wanted to tell me this many times. I felt it but I avoided her. My sister also wanted to speak to me but I avoided her too. I knew well that if I left Diaghilev I would die of hunger because I was not ready for life. I was afraid of life. Now I am not afraid any more. I wait for God's wishes.

Death

When I went upstairs it was already five o'clock.
I went into my dressing room and changed. Going
upstairs I thought: "Where is my wife? In the bedroom where I sleep or in another one?"* And I felt
my body trembling. I trembled as I tremble now. I
cannot write because I am trembling with cold. I
cannot write. I am correcting this, for I am afraid
my handwriting will be illegible. When I went into
the bedroom I felt cold before I saw anything. Her
bed was without the pillows and the covers were
folded back. I went downstairs having decided not
to go to sleep. I wanted to finish writing down my
impressions. I cannot write, for I feel cold in every
part of my body. I ask God to help me because my
hand is aching and it is difficult to write. I want to
write well.

My wife is not asleep and I am also awake. She
thinks and I feel. I am afraid for her. I do not know
what to tell her tomorrow. I will talk to no one tomorrow. Tomorrow I will sleep. I want to write but
cannot. I think. I am so cold that I cannot write. My
fingers are beginning to stiffen. I want to say that
she does not love me. I am so sad. My heart is heavy.
I know that people get used to sadness and also I
will get used to it, but I am afraid to get used to sad-

*At this time, on account of Nijinsky's nervous condition, he and
his wife slept sometimes in separate rooms.

[109]

ness because I know it is death. I will ask my wife's forgiveness, but she will not understand me because she will think that I was in the wrong. Her mind will grow cold. I am freezing and cannot write, for my fingers are getting stiff. I am sorry for myself and for her, and I cry. I am getting cold. I do not feel any more. I am dying.

I want to sleep but God does not wish it. I pity myself and people like me. Everyone will say that I am a wicked man, but I do not wish to harm people —it is they who want to harm me.

I got up at three o'clock today, but awoke earlier. I heard people talking but did not know who they were. I understood much later, recognizing the voices. My wife's mother and her husband. They had arrived. I waited to see what God would tell me to do. I did not do anything and was bored. In that hour I understood more than anyone else would learn and understand in a whole lifetime. I thought with God and knew that God loved me, therefore I was not afraid to do as He wanted me to. I was afraid of death and was sad. I was sorry for my wife. She cried and I suffered. God wanted me to suffer, and to understand the meaning of death. I understood it and waited for God's commands. I did not know whether to get up or stay in bed. God will not hurt me. My soul has suffered. I wanted to cry. I heard my wife sobbing, then her laugh. I heard my wife's mother threatening. My soul was crying. I looked on the wall and saw the wallpaper, then at the lamp and saw glass, into the distance and saw emptiness. I cried and felt sad. I did not know what to do. I wanted to console my wife but God did not want me to, I wanted to laugh but stopped because I had felt death. I heard what they were saying about me and understood what they were all thinking. I felt bored. I wanted to cheer them up, but I lay down. My soul cried. I tremble when people do not understand me. I feel a great deal. The fire inside me does not go out. I live with God. I came here to help—I want paradise on earth. At the moment earth is an inferno. When people quarrel—it is an inferno. Yesterday I quarreled with my wife. I did it to make her a better person—I was not angry and annoyed her, to kindle her love for me. I want to inflame the earth and people, not to extinguish them. Scientists extinguish the fire of the earth and the love of people for each other. If people only had more pity for each other, life would last longer.

People think that children are necessary in order to have soldiers. They kill children and cover the earth with ashes. I am a Russian and therefore I know what earth is. I cannot plow, but I know that the earth is warm and that without its warmth there would be no bread. Man is born strong—he weakens himself because he does not take care of his life. I want love. Love is life and laughter death. Many people will say: "Why does Nijinsky always speak of God? He has gone mad—he is a dancer and nothing else." I understand all these sneers and they do not make me angry. I weep and weep. Many people will say that Nijinsky is always weeping. I am not. I am alive and therefore suffer, but I rarely shed tears. My soul is weeping.

Without energy there is no life. Life is difficult, because men do not know the importance of it. Life is short. I do not write to amuse myself, but to make men understand life and death. I love life. I love death. Death can be lovely when it is God's wish, dreadful when it is without God. My wife's father shot himself. He studied a great deal and became neurotic because his brain was overworked. I do not study much, only when God wishes me to study. God does not want men to overtax themselves. He wants men to be happy. . . .

Men waste so much. They think that the more one has, the happier one is, but the fewer possessions one has, the more peaceful and happy one feels. I cannot write—my feeling has attracted my wife to me. I love her! She read the things I have written and understood me. I told her not to disturb me when I am writing and she went out without feeling sad about it. She seems to be more sensitive today and I am happy because I hope that she will improve. My wife's mother is no longer agitated, because she sees that I love my wife.

I do not like egoism, and want to live simply, and everybody to be happy. I would be the happiest man if I found that everyone gets an equal share. I shall be the happiest man when I am able to act and dance without getting any money, or any other pay, for it. I am afraid of clever people and freeze when a clever man is near me. There is a cold atmosphere around him. I do not write to argue or reason, but to explain. I want to help mankind, and am not boasting about my book, because I do not know how to write. People will understand my thoughts if this book is well published. I do not wish to earn but my wife needs money because she is afraid of life. I am not, but I have no right to leave my wife without means.

Emma, my wife's mother, and Oscar, her husband, are good people. I love them but, like everyone else, they have their faults. I will describe their faults so that they should read about them and become better people. I want them to see me at work. I like people who work. Emma and Oscar are tired after their long journey. They thought that I was insane but have seen that it is not so. Oscar realized that I understand politics and therefore he is interested in me. He likes politics and financial affairs and business, but I dislike these things. I like him but he thinks too much.

I do not think that timidity and fear are faults. People who are afraid are usually good people. Some people pretend that they are not afraid. Many say that fear is a weakness. People will say that I do not know what fear is because I did not fight in the war —but I fought for life, not in the trenches but at home. I fought with my wife's mother when I was interned in Hungary. People say that I lived very well because I lived in the house of my wife's mother. I lived well—I was not hungry but my soul suffered. I like solitude. I worked on some ballets because I had nothing to do. I felt sad. I know that everybody disliked me. My wife's mother Emma pretended that she loved me. I tried to explain to her my feelings. She did not understand me, she thought that I was wicked. I was not, I was a martyr. I cried, thinking my wife did not understand me. Oscar did not understand me either. He thought about money because it was difficult for them to keep us. My mother-in-law had to feed me without being paid for it because I was a relation. Relations usually dislike each other, and so I decided to pretend that I was offended. She did not understand me. She thought that I was a poor man and was afraid I would cost money. I know the meaning and value of money but like to think it is not important.

I knew the value of money when I was a child. My mother used to give me fifty kopecks a week for sweets. She used to earn money by letting rooms, and by her doing this we were able to get food. I ate a great deal as I was always hungry, not understanding that I should have been eating less. I used to eat like a grown-up person although I was only twelve years old. When I stayed at my mother-in-law's house I had a good appetite. Food was very expensive on account of the war. Emma, my wife's mother, was a nervous woman. She liked me because of my success with the public. She liked my dances. I did not want to dance then because I was sad and interned. I realized that one could live anywhere. I was working on a system of notation for dancing and under the table the cats were making a mess. I disliked the cats because of their filth, hating filth. I did not realize that in reality it was not the cats who were making the mess, but the people. I looked after the cats and cared only for my system of dancing. I wanted to forget myself and so started to write down my ballet

*Faun** by this system. It was a long job—it took me two months, and it took only ten minutes to perform this ballet itself. Again I felt sad and miserable. I cried because I was so depressed. Without realizing it, I felt sad and dull about life. I read Tolstoy. Reading was a rest, but I did not understand the meaning of life. I lived from one day to the other and used to do my dancing exercises. I started developing my muscles. My muscles became strong but my dances were not good. I felt this was death to my dancing and became nervous, anxious, and so did my wife's mother. We were both anxious and nervous. I did not like her and quarreled about every trifle. I dislike pettiness but quarreled because I had nothing else to do. I lived from day to day. My wife was bored. I realized that people would not understand me if I disapproved of their actions, and decided to pretend these people understood me.

I am sometimes afraid to enter a public bar or a flat because I think God does not wish it. Once I passed a public bar which God wished me to enter, but I felt a lassitude in my body and the feeling of death in my mind. Though I wanted to enter, God stopped me. People will say, "What is Nijinsky talking about? He keeps on saying that God wishes and

Nijinsky is referring to his ballet L'APRÈS-MIDI D'UN FAUNE.

[116]

orders him to do this and that and he himself does
nothing at all." I am not an ordinary man. I love
God and He loves me. I want everybody to be like
myself. I am not a spiritualist, not a medium. I am a
man in God. I am afraid of perfection because I am
afraid people will not understand me. My life is a
sacrifice because I do not live like others. I work all
day. I love work and want everyone to work as I
work.

My life in Budapest during the war was sad. I
lived for a long time in my mother-in-law's house,
not knowing what to do. It was dull, I was bored.
When I found out that I was going to be liberated
soon, I felt courageous and strong and decided to
escape from my mother-in-law's house. I went with
my wife and child to a hotel because I had received
some money. I was not angry with my mother-in-
law, and I loved her because I knew it was hard for
her to keep us. She saw her mistake and came running to the hotel to beseech us to come back. We
did not agree to this, knowing we would be going
away soon, and said good-by to my mother-in-law
and thanked her for her hospitality. Oscar always
used to voice his opinions in a loud tone; I was offended and nearly fought with him, but my wife
stopped me and her mother stopped Oscar. We quarreled about politics. Oscar said that Russia was in

the wrong and I said that Russia was right. I provoked Oscar. Many people will not believe what I say, but I do not mind because I know that many others will see the truth in it. I spoke no more to Oscar and left without saying good-by. I had caught them unawares. They thought about it and changed their attitude. They understood me because I was a clever actor. I pretended because I wished them well. I loved them but I had to act and play up to it all, and therefore was angry. My anger was also pretense, for I loved them. Romola's mother was a difficult woman. She had her own habits and ways.

My mother-in-law got angry with her husband out of jealousy. I was sorry for Oscar because I saw he looked at the maid out of curiosity, and therefore I defended him. I thought at first that he flirted with the maids but realized that it was only Emma's imagination. Oscar loved her and always defended her. I saw that his soul was crying and felt sorry for him, but did not tell him anything because I thought he would not understand me. Now I understand him and hope he will love me. I gave him several of my drawings because I saw he liked them.

People will copy me but imitation is not life, it is death. Many people say that Raphael and Andrea del Sarto used to copy and that Andrea del Sarto copied the *Gioconda* so that one cannot tell who painted

[118]

it: Andrea del Sarto or Leonardo da Vinci. I think
that Raphael copied pictures because he needed to
improve his technique. I like technique but I do not
like imitation. I do not like copies, and so I do not
want to be copied. My drawings are simple and easy
to copy. I do not like signing my drawings because I
know that no one will be able to do what I have
done. I know there will be many who will copy me
but I will do everything to make it impossible. Copy-
ists remind me of monkeys, because monkeys imitate
human beings. A monkey imitates, but does not understand; it is a stupid animal.

This morning I showed them what my nerves are
like and everybody was frightened. I suddenly began
to sing like Chaliapin in a low voice. I love Chaliapin—he is sensitive and feels his songs and his acting. People interfere in his development, asking him
to act and sing things he does not like; he can act
well even in plays he does not like. He is a great
artist and can act in any part.

I will behave like others because I want people to
take care of me. I am not an egoist, but a man of
love, and will do everything possible for other people. I want to be looked after. I hope that people
will love my wife and my child but I want love for
everybody. I want to act in plays which will interest
the public because I know that people like to be

pleased, but in this excitement I will make people feel what love is. I do not want people to love spiritual death, and to be afraid of death which comes from God. I want people to improve and do not want the death of the spirit. I am a dove. People think when they look at icons and see the dove, but they do not understand the church and go there from habit, being afraid of God. God is not in icons, but in the soul of man. Many will say: "Nijinsky has gone mad, he is a dancer, a comedian." But people will love me when they see my life in this house. Everybody is afraid to trouble me, they think they would bother me, but I do not get bothered, worried. I am a man of love. I love the *moujik*, the Tsar, everybody. I make no distinctions. I do not belong to a party. I am the love of God. I know my wife's faults and therefore want to help her to improve herself. Many will say, "Nijinsky tyrannizes and bullies his wife and everybody else." I will feel sorry for these people because of their mistake, and weep like Christ. I am not Christ; I am Nijinsky, a simple man. I have bad habits but I want to get rid of them. People should tell me my faults—I want them to take care of me. I will take care of others. I want loving and not ill-intentioned care—I do not want indulgence.

God will help me, as I understand Him. I am a

man with faults—and know that everyone has faults. God wants to help everybody—I can feel God. If people would feel my thoughts, God would help them all. I see through people. They do not have to tell me about themselves—I can understand them without words. They will say: "How can you know me when you have not even seen me?" But I can, I can feel and think. My mind is so developed that I understand people without talking to them. I see their deeds and understand everything. I understand everything. I am a *moujik*, a workman, a factory worker, a servant, a master, an aristocrat, the Tsar. God. I am God. I am God. I am all, life, infinity. I will be always and everywhere. I can be killed but will live because I am all. I want infinite life, not death. I also have faults. I am not a comedian, an actor. Come and look at me and you will see that I am a man with faults, but I shall have no more faults when people begin to help me. I want to see people and therefore my doors are always open, my cupboards and trunks always unlocked. Should you find my door locked, ring the bell and I will open it if I am at home. I love my wife and want her to be happy but she does not yet understand me or my needs, and therefore she tells the servants to shut my door. My wife will feel nervous if people start rushing into my house, and therefore I ask everybody to remain at home and wait for me. I will come to those who call me. I will be there without being there. I am the spirit in every man. I will go if God orders me to go but I will not go if people say: "Come to me." I will listen to men but I will not go to them because I do not want to start a revolt. I do not like death. I want death. I want men to feel me. I love God. I love life, everybody, and I do everything I can for other people. I do not like the constant begging of favors or the societies of relief for the poor. Everybody is poor. I will help spiritually. I want spiritual love, not physical. I like the physical body because it is necessary for the spirit.

I do not want people to be forced to read my book, but should like them to read it and to go to the theater and see me dance because they will feel inspired. I want theaters to be free of charge. I know that nowadays one cannot do anything without money and therefore I will work hard so that people can come and see my dancing free. I also will work hard to make money because I have to show people that I am not poor, but rich. Nowadays people think that a man who has no money is stupid and lazy, and so I will make money in spite of my feelings and then only will I show people what I really am. I want to publish these two books so that people may understand my behavior and all my actions. I want to

work alone because I can earn money quicker working by myself; also I am going to gamble on the
Stock Exchange. I will do everything to get rich because I know the value of money. I will go to Zurich
with Oscar and there gamble, buying shares which
I consider to be good. Oscar will get frightened, thinking I might lose. He will implore me not to do it.
Rockefeller is a good man—he gives money to people but he does not understand the meaning of money
because he gives it to science. I will give my money
to love, to this divine feeling of God that is in man.
I will buy theaters and will dance for people gratu-
itously. Those who want to pay will have to wait
their turn to get seats and those who cannot pay will
decide amicably who is to go in first. I want people
to arrange it in a friendly way. If things are done in
an unjust way I will ask the culprit to leave the
theater, and ask those who have been cheated to
come to me. I can see at once by a man's face whether
he has cheated because I am a physiognomist. I will
show everybody that I know and understand. Come
to me and you will see! Some people make use of
ambition for the benefit of the rich alone. I make use
of ambition for the benefit of every class. I am not a
liberal—I don't belong to a party. I belong to God
and do everything He commands me to do. Many
will ask, "Which God commands you to do all you

are doing? You are deceiving us. You are a primitive man without any culture." I know all these statements. I am a man with the culture of God, not with that of man. I do not want death. I want men to live. I do not consider egotism and foul actions to be culture. I love the working classes, the rich and the poor, everybody—love must be equal. I do not want servants only to work for money. My servants love me. At the beginning I quarreled with them. Many say that servants are fools and that if one does not show a fist they will not understand you. I also have treated servants in this way, but today I have understood that I am not right in treating them like this. Servants must not suffer. Servants are not ungrateful, they are human beings as well as we are, only less intelligent. Servants feel it when they are not loved, and therefore resent this. Some say that servants have no right to feel angry because they are paid. But a maid is paid with money which belongs to her, because she works for it. People forget that money is not more important than work. Nowadays everybody notices that work is dearer than money because there are not enough working people. I am a workingman. Everybody ought to work, but all work is not equal. Good work is needed. I work also writing these books. I do not write for my own pleasure—there can be no pleasure when a man spends all his free time on writing. One has to write a great deal to be able to understand what writing means. It is a difficult occupation—one gets tired of sitting, having the legs cramped, the arm stiff. It spoils the eyes and one does not get enough air; the room gets stuffy. From such a life a man dies sooner. People who write at night spoil their eyes and have to wear glasses, the hypocrites use monocles. I notice that from writing a long time my eyes get bloodshot. People who write a great deal are martyrs. I like martyrs for the sake of God. Many say one should write for money, for without money one cannot live. With tears in my eyes I see that these people are like Christ crucified. I weep when I hear such things, as I have experienced it in another manner by dancing for money. I nearly died because I was so exhausted. I was like a horse, which is being forced with a whip to drag a heavy load. Carriers whipped their horses to death, because they did not understand that the animals had no more strength left. The coachman drove the horse downhill, using his whip. The horse fell—I saw it and my soul was crying. I wanted to sob aloud but thought that people would take me for a weakling and therefore wept inwardly. The horse was lying on its side and cried from pain. I felt it. The veterinary surgeon shot this horse with a revolver out of pity.

I met a French sportsman, Monsieur R. I told him

that his dog was very beautiful, but with sadness in his voice, he told me that he would shoot that dog because he felt that it would be better for it to die than suffer from hunger. I realized that he had no money and wanted to help him. I knew that he was an ambitious man, he wanted to win silver cups in the skeleton run. Skeleton running is the sport when a man lies face-down on a sleigh made of steel and uses all his strength to make it go faster. Such speed is very dangerous and many sportsmen are killed at it. These are often affected by drinking and smoking and therefore their nerves are easily upset. They go down the *piste* at full speed, get nervous and kill themselves. I told Monsieur R. this, and he agreed, for he had once fallen during a race and nearly died. I told him that I thought he was nervous today, that he had a sorrow. I noticed tears in his eyes, but I did not let him know, for I was afraid that he might start crying. He told me that he would shoot his dog. He seemed depressed and I cried inwardly. He felt that I loved the dog and went away, leaving my wife and me.

We were lunching together with the doctor who has been invited by my wife. He was watching me, wanting to know whether I was mentally deranged or not. He is certain that "something is definitely wrong" with me. I know that something is wrong

Blue and red ink picture made by Nijinsky while in the asylum

Water-color made by Nijinsky while in the asylum

with him; he is a nervous man. He smokes a lot; he
got into this habit at school. I believe that many
people only smoke because they want to look important. Some people when they smoke look very dignified and proud. I went to visit the mayor of St.
Moritz, Mr. G. I wanted to cheer them up and therefore came in to have a chat. Oscar started to talk to
the mayor. He assumed a dignified air and so did
Oscar, and they started to smoke. I was looking
through the telescope at the mountains, because I
was told one could see the stags. I looked and did not
see anything, and told Mr. G. that I preferred not to
look any more as I came to see the host, not the stags.
They laughed, but I felt they were not interested in
me, they were interested in Oscar; so I left them and
started looking for the stags again. I fixed the telescope and looking through I saw a stag; he was not
frightened of me looking at him—I saw him well. It
was an old fat stag. I told them that the stag had
turned its back. I wanted them to feel I was there,
but they had no time for me. I told Oscar that we
should be going, as the soup was ready for us at
home. Mr. G. and his wife laughed, but they had no
time for me, they were thinking, not feeling. I felt
hurt—they thought that I was mad, but when the
hostess asked me how my health was I replied that I

was always very well and at this she smiled. I felt hurt and I cried inwardly.

Having nothing better to do, my mother-in-law, my wife, and Oscar came into the drawing room. My wife asked me to show my drawings but I pretended I did not want to. I showed them the drawings they had already seen. My wife asked me to show the other drawings too. I took up a packet at which I had been working ceaselessly for a period of two or three months and threw these drawings on the floor. My mother-in-law, my wife, and Oscar realized that I did not like my drawings. I told them that nobody was interested in them and therefore I took them off the wall. They said they were very sorry and started to look at them. I explained the meaning of these drawings to them.

The Parisians may understand me, for they are sensitive. They said that they also understood my drawings. I did not reply. I showed them some of my drawings because I wanted them to feel, but realized that they could only think, and left them, crying inwardly. I have a soul and therefore I weep when I see that people do not understand me. I knew I would not be understood and took off all the drawings from the walls of my room and hid them in the lower part of the top of the piano. I knew also that nobody would understand my manuscript, but I thought that the doctor would take it for a time to be translated. I did not want to show my manuscripts, being certain that the doctor would not understand me and would think that I was insane. I was afraid for my wife and so I hid my books, also all the drawings of my scenery, because I feel they will not understand. I do not want to raise any ill feelings while my mother-in-law is here, for I do not want her to take my wife away with her. I have no money and am afraid that I will be put into an asylum. I see what people are driving at without being told. I feel disgusted, not angry but disgusted. I am afraid of Oscar and Emma. They are both dead for me.

I want to help Oscar because I noticed that he understands me.

I realize that paper will get dearer, and therefore I will buy a big quantity of it in Zurich because I want to work hard; people are wicked and will not give me what I need, and therefore I must provide and care for myself. God has shown me His care. He wants me to work out the problem He has given me. He often tells me that I will lose but I am sure I will win in order that the problems which God puts before us may be settled.

I will go to Zurich tomorrow with Oscar, my wife, and my mother-in-law.

I do not like wicked people. I have written down

the name of Diaghielev, etc., etc., because it is easier for people to notice these names. I purposely made a mistake just now in writing the word Diaghilev because I want him to see that I have forgotten how to spell his name.

I wanted to continue to write on the previous line, but God does not wish me to go on writing on the line where the name of Diaghilev is written. I have noticed my mistake, I had written the name of God and of Diaghilev with a capital. I will write god with a small letter because I want no similarity. . . .

I want to go away because I am tired of sitting. But I will go alone if no one notices me. Everybody will think that I am still working. I will go out into the street through the back door, and walk up high, and I will look down because I want to feel the height I am reaching. . . .

I came out in the street by the back door and felt the cold. The others are sitting in the dining room, therefore I passed noiselessly. People have nothing to do and therefore they interfere with the life of others. I do not want to interfere with the life of others. I walked out of the house, because I felt that there I am not loved. I met the doctor, he looked bored. I shook his hand, but before that I said, "Everybody is ill." My soul felt cold and empty and therefore I walked out. Oscar came to me and asked me to come in for tea. Oscar felt that the doctor was hurt and wanted to make peace between us. I did not want to make peace—I stopped him.

I told Oscar the object of my great work, explaining that I do not get tired from working. It seemed to me that he understood me, he agreed to what I said. Oscar quickly agrees to what I say. I wanted to prove to him that writing inspired by God does not tire. . . .

I had tea with the doctor, Oscar, my mother-in-law, and my wife. I was having tea quietly, but after some time I became interested in the conversation and made them feel merry. I did it with a purpose and said things that everybody understood. I joked. Everybody felt merry but I noticed that the doctor thought that I wanted to laugh at him. So I changed the conversation. I talked about the Bolsheviks in Russia. I wanted to tell something, but God wanted my wife to do so. She could not tell it, because she did not feel Him. I helped her to remember. I did not want to speak much, but God wanted me to interest everybody. I did this and went away, because I thought I was not wanted. The doctor is leaving and I am remaining. I do not want to see him off, as I want him to feel that nobody here wants his medical assistance. . . .

He came to say good-by to me and I shook his

hand. He asked me not to write too much. I told him not to worry about me. He asked me whether I would like to see a specialist in Zurich. I replied that I did not know, but if my wife should wish it, I would see him. He assured me that it would be a very good thing if I would see this professor, as he is very great. I told him that I would go and see him if this would calm my wife. The doctor understood me. I shook his hand.

My head is beginning to ache, because I ate a lot. I eat a lot because I do not want my wife's mother to think that I am mean. She feels that I am not. Oscar loves me and is worried about my health. He has been told that it is bad for me to work a lot. I know why people get tired. I feel sick, my head aches. I will eat little this evening and I know that then in the morning I will feel better. . . .

I am going to Zurich at seven o'clock in the morning, and will go to bed early so that this specialist shall see me in good condition. I will talk to him about nerves because this subject interests me. I am not going to do any writing in Zurich, because I am very interested in this town. I will go to a bordel because I want to understand cocottes. I want to understand the psychology of a cocotte. I will go to several if God orders me. I know that God does not like this, but I know that He wants to try me. I feel great

[132]

spiritual strength and therefore will not make a mistake. I will give money to the cocottes, but will do
nothing with them. I feel sexual excitement and, at
the same time, fear. The blood rushes to my head
and I feel that if I go on thinking I shall have a fit.
I know about apoplectic fits. My friend Serge Botkin
cured me of typhoid fever in Paris, during the year of
my debut. I drank water from a jug, because I was
poor and could not buy mineral water, drank very
quickly without suspecting the danger. I went to
dance and, returning home* in the evening, felt a
great weakness in my body. Diaghilev called Dr. Botkin—he knew him well. Serge Botkin was one of the
Tsar's doctors. I felt feverish but I was not afraid,
not realizing what was the matter with me. Serge
Botkin saw me and looked at me and understood
what had happened. I got frightened, noticing that
the doctor and Diaghilev were looking at each other.
They understood without words, so did I. Botkin
looked at my breast and saw a rash. I got frightened,
as he became very nervous and called Diaghilev to
come into the other room. This hotel has been pulled
down now. It was a poor hotel, but on the little
money I had I could not live in a better way. In this
hotel Diaghilev made me an offer to live with him

*Hôtel de Hollande, Avenue de l'Opéra, now demolished.

when I was lying ill in a high fever. I agreed. Diaghilev realized my value and therefore was afraid that I would leave him; at that time I wanted to run away. I was twenty years old. I was frightened of life. I did not know then that I was part of God. I wept and wept, and I did not know what to do. I was afraid of life, my mother was also afraid of life, and I had inherited this fear from her. I did not want to agree. Diaghilev was sitting on my bed and urged me to do so. I was frightened of him, frightened, and I agreed. I sobbed and sobbed; I had understood death. I could not run away as I had fever. I was alone. I was eating an orange; I was thirsty and asked Diaghilev to give me an orange and he brought me some. I fell asleep with the orange in my hand; when I woke up, it was squashed and lying on the floor. I slept for a long time, not understanding what was happening to me. I lost consciousness. I was afraid of Diaghilev, not of death. I realized that I had typhoid fever, as I had already had it in my childhood—I remembered that people recognize it by spots on the body.

My wife came and kissed me. I felt happy but God did not want me to show my joy to my wife because He wants her to change. . . .

Botkin died. I saw his body from the distance; he was lying on a catafalque. I understood death—God frightened me—and I went away without kissing his body. Everybody kissed it, but I could not look at the whole procedure. Relations wept and friends pretended to be sad. They looked round the apartment and at the pictures trying to make out their value. After his death all his belongings were sold, because Serge Botkin's wife did not like her husband's refined taste. Serge Botkin bought pictures because people told him that one should buy old masters. His apartment was full of them. People are not interested in modern pictures, thinking that they are not truly artistic. They buy old pictures to show their love for art. I realized that people love art, but are afraid to say to themselves: "I don't understand art." People are cowards because the critics frighten them. They frighten people to make them ask their opinion. The critics believe that the public is stupid. They think that they have to explain pictures to the public, and think that without them there would be no art. The public would not understand works of art which have not been seen by the critics. I know what criticism means—it is death.

Once I talked to a man on a steamer, traveling from New York to Boston. It was a heated conversation; he had aroused me. He was a Russian political spy, and he thought I was an anarchist. I do not know why he thought this. He had a nasty face and did not

like me. I felt this and decided to be careful with him.
He started a conversation in order to provoke my
opinion about internal politics. I realized it and decided to annoy him by explaining the question which
he had asked. I spoke loudly, wanting to impress
him. He thought that I was getting irritated and pretended to be himself; his face was not alive when he
spoke to me; he pretended to be nervous. I realized
that I was a better actor than he, and began to talk
to him about critics and criticism. He listened, being
tired of contradicting; then he interrupted me and
wanted to change the conversation but I did not. He
was displeased and became fidgety. As I noticed that
he disliked my conversation I left him without finishing what I wanted to say about critics. I found out
later that he had asked my wife whether I was a
Nihilist. I do not know what a Nihilist or Nihilism is.
I was educated at the Imperial School of Dancing,
where they did not teach the meaning of such words.
I was a pupil of the Imperial School, and did not
hear about politics until I married. I had to learn
about it then, as I was afraid of life and I had to live.
Criticism is unnecessary. Some people feel it is necessary because without it they would not be able to
judge what is good and what is bad. Critics write because they need money; nowadays one cannot live
without it. Critics work hard, but they do not really

work for the sake of art. They only write about it.
An artist gives all his life up to art. The critics will
tear an artist to pieces if they do not like his work.
People say that the critics are not prejudiced, but
they are egoists. They write their own opinion, not
what the public feels. Applause is not opinion—it is
the expression of love the public feels for the artist. I
love applause and know its value. The critics do not
understand applause. They like to criticize because
they want to show that they are cleverer than the
public. In Paris the public does not listen to the critics. Therefore they are annoyed, as they cannot influence the public. Calmette* was a well-known critic
—he also wrote about politics. He gave a very base
review of *Faun*, saying that it was dissolute. When I
composed this ballet, I was not thinking of perversity.
I loved creating it. I created the whole ballet alone.
I also gave the idea for the scenery, but Leon Bakst
did not understand what I wanted. The creation of
this ballet took a long time but I worked well, feeling
the presence of God. I loved this ballet and therefore
I made the public love it too. Rodin wrote a good
criticism about *Faun*, but he was influenced: he wrote
a criticism at the request of Diaghilev. Rodin is a
rich man; he was not in need of money. He was in-

Owner and editor of the FIGARO.

fluenced and was asked to write—he had never written criticisms before. He was upset and nervous because he did not like writing.

He wanted to make a drawing of me, wishing to make a marble statue of me. He looked at my naked body and found that it was perfect, and therefore destroyed his sketches. I felt he liked me and went away. Calmette wrote his own criticism the same day. I understood, hearing Diaghilev's conversation with Bakst, that Calmette had been laughed at by the public. Calmette lost the public's belief in him as a critic of the theater. . . .

Svetlov, a critic on a Petersburg newspaper, wrote under Calmette's influence. Diaghilev had wanted him to come and assist him in managing the Russian Ballet, but Svetlov thought that the Russian Ballet was a failure, and therefore hurried to inform the Russian public of this, fearing that other newspapers would get hold of the news before him. Svetlov usually read the *Figaro* and must have received the paper before he left St. Petersburg. He was not in the habit of reading the French newspaper *Le Matin* —he therefore did not know of Rodin's criticism. Had he known about it, I am certain he would not have written like Calmette; he would have listened to Rodin. I noticed how nervous Svetlov was upon his arrival in Paris. He realized that he had made a mistake and he avoided me. I was not afraid of him because he was nasty to me. I am not afraid of people like this, but fight against them. Naturally I was up against him and did not bow to him. He pretended that he did not like my ballets, but he no longer wrote about me. He wrote the *History of the Ballet* without knowing it. He did not even mention my existence in this book. He ignored me. I was saddened, for I had worked a great deal for the Russian Ballet. Diaghilev was furious but did not show it. Svetlov wrote this book on purpose to show Diaghilev that he did not follow Calmette's criticism. Svetlov saw that everybody was laughing at him and to justify himself he wrote this book.

I loved Karsavina. She excited me a little, because she was beautifully made, but one could not flirt with her and therefore I felt exasperated. I courted her in Paris. My courtship was such as to make her feel that she attracted me. She felt this, but did not respond because she was married. I felt I had made a mistake and kissed her hand. She understood that I wanted nothing from her and felt happy. I know Karsavina well because I worked with her for five years. I was young and did many stupid things. I used to quarrel with Karsavina and did not want to ask her forgiveness because I felt hurt. I realized that Diaghilev influenced her against me as he noticed that I was attracted by her. Karsavina made use of a trifle to start a quarrel, and I was very irritated, weeping bitterly because I loved Karsavina also as a woman. She felt I had offended her and cried too.

I felt weak and could not go on composing the ballet *Jeux*.* It was a ballet about flirting, and unsuccessful, as I had no feeling for it. I started it well but then people began to hurry me and I could not finish it properly. The story of this ballet is about three young men making love to each other. I began to understand life when I was twenty-two years old. I composed this ballet alone, too. Debussy, the well-known composer, wanted the subject to be written down. I asked Diaghilev to help me to do this and with Bakst they wrote it down on paper. I told Diaghilev my idea.

Diaghilev likes to say that he created the ballet, because he likes to be praised. I do not mind if Diaghilev says that he composed the stories of *Faun* and *Jeux* because when I created them I was under the influence of "my life" with Diaghilev. The *Faun* is me, and *Jeux* is the life of which Diaghilev dreamed. He wanted to have two boys as lovers. He often told me so, but I refused. Diaghilev wanted to make love to two boys at the same time, and wanted these boys

---

*JEUX, *choreography by Nijinsky, music by Debussy, was produced in Paris in 1913.*

to make love to him. In the ballet, the two girls represent the two boys and the young man is Diaghilev. I changed the characters, as love between three men could not be represented on the stage. I wanted people to feel as disgusted with the idea of evil love as I did, but I could not finish the ballet. Debussy did not like the subject either, but he was paid 10,000 gold francs for this ballet and therefore had to finish it. . . .

I know that tomorrow I must go to Zurich and so I will go to bed. . . .

I did not go to bed; I have a headache and indigestion. I do not like having such pain and want it to stop. I asked God to help me and He told me not to go to bed. I will sleep in the train because I am fed up with Oscar and my mother-in-law, although they have been here only one day. I do not want to speak to them. I told my wife this, but so that her mother should hear it; I must finish my work, as in Zurich I can't go on with my writing. My wife understood me and did not reply, but I do not know what her mother thought—I did not see her face. I noticed it today at lunch. I gave her a tangerine which had been left for me. She wanted a second one, so I gave her mine, and said that I did not mind having an orange instead. She took it and did not say anything. I showed her I was not pleased. Oscar started to defend her; I took the tangerine back, giving half of it to Oscar and the other half to my wife. My wife refused, thinking I wanted it. I put it back later on my mother-in-law's plate but she did not eat it, neither did she say anything. She felt my reproach, but showed no sign of it. She reminds me of Diaghilev. She is a very good actress and so knows how to pretend. I understand acting.

My mother-in-law is a great artist. I know this as I myself am an actor, but I know her as a woman also. Already in Budapest when I was interned I saw that she knew how to be a hypocrite in life.

I do not want to be told to go to bed,* and I will go only when God orders me to. I told my wife that I would come soon, but I will go on writing for a long time. I dislike being disturbed when I work. I know what is good for me, and ask to be helped, not to be disturbed. . . .

I do not like to quarrel with the servants. I like to share. My wife's mother does not like servants, because they show her their will, and she does not understand them. I love servants and do what they like, but I do not want to spoil them. I am not the kind of person who spoils others.

I want to write about the life of my wife's mother. People will say that I am a comedian just as she is,

---

Nijinsky was called to bed by his wife.

the only difference being that she is a woman, a dramatic actress, and I am a man and a dancer. People do not trust dancers and so I want to explain what a dancer is. . . . I love my mother-in-law as a human being, but I do not like her for the way she behaves in life. She is not very sensitive.

The nerves in my head hurt me. I feel my blood has rushed from my head. I feel death near me. I do not want death and I ask God to help me. . . . I should like to write beautifully, because I can feel beauty. My mother-in-law used to be a beautiful woman, but she spoiled her loveliness as she was always angry; she was always having bilious attacks. I used to tell her when I was in Budapest that she had these attacks because she was always quarreling and shouting at people. She did not believe me—she does not believe anybody. She seems to like poor, simple people, and gives her hand to conductors. She does it in an uneasy way which makes the conductors blush and feel awkward, because they think she is laughing at them. She is a good woman because she cries when she sees people who have been hurt. People say that she is charitable when she finds work for an unemployed person.

I used to think myself for a long time that she was a good woman but I have noticed quite by accident that she does not love my wife. The first day of our

acquaintance she wanted to influence me and therefore showed me some old photographs of herself and
of my wife.* My wife started to cry, because she felt
very hurt. I also felt offended and went away. From
that day, I no longer trusted my mother-in-law. She
felt that I was strong because I took no notice of her.
I quarreled with her because she aggravated me. She
was afraid that I would speak badly of her, and so
she used to tell people that I was a horrible man and
that I disliked her. I realized that she had said nasty
things about me, as people started to turn their back
on me—those who used to embrace me no longer
greeted me. My mother-in-law was overjoyed. She
thought she had won the battle. I was not conquered
—I was not angry with her. I pretended to be angry
only because I wanted to make her a better woman.
I showed her my will every day. She doubled her
fury—I trebled mine, and in this manner we quarreled for eighteen months—those terrible months
when I was interned. I do not like nasty people and
therefore I want to disarm them by writing about
their life. I want my mother-in-law to realize how
she has hurt people and to ask their forgiveness. I
know that all the Hungarian critics will be roused
and that I will be torn to pieces, but I will ask God

* *These were photos in which the mother looked lovely and the daughter looked sick; she was at an awkward age.*

to disarm the critics. I will reply to them if God orders me to. I know that people will understand me and I will thank God for His love.

I know that He loves me and will help me in everything. I am poor—I am a pauper. I have not a roof over my head and no food—I have nothing. My mother-in-law has a house with three stories and marble columns. She likes this house, but I do not like it because it is built in an awkward way, though there are many lovely old pictures and Gobelins in it. I like nothing that is old, because old things smell of death. I like old people, but I do not like the spirit to be old. My spirit is young. Tolstoy had a young spirit, so had Beethoven and Wagner. I love everybody. I wrote about Tolstoy because he is a part of God. Wagner, Beethoven, also.

I am going away to Zurich. I do not want to do anything before my departure. Everybody is nervous. The maids have become stupid because they do not feel God. I feel Him, but I have not become stupid. I do not want to crack, but to say the truth. Oscar is telephoning to Zurich. He is afraid that people will not understand his name. He feels that nobody knows his name there and so he wants to make them understand it. His name is Pardany, and he pronounces it with an accent on every syllable. I do not care whether people know my name or not, and

I am not afraid that people will not love me if they find out that I am poor.

When I was at school I used to shut myself in, pretending I was ill, so that I could read. I used to lie down and read, quietly. I want to write about the departure for Zurich, everybody is nervous because I did not care. I thought this journey was absurd, but I will go because God wants it. But if He did not wish it, I would remain. I am beginning to understand God. I know that He creates movement, and so I ask Him to help me.

I want to write about the journey. The whole thing was called off because everybody forgot what time the train went. Oscar, my mother-in-law, and my wife relied on Louise, who forgot the hour of departure that the man at the station had told her. She forgot it because she was nervous. My wife and my mother-in-law were furious with her. I explained to them laughingly that it was not her fault, but I saw my mother-in-law looking at me. I said that the time-table was often changed on account of the war. My mother-in-law thought I wanted to defend Louise, and I changed the conversation because I did not want to start a quarrel. My mother-in-law and my wife are in a bad temper. Oscar is nervous. I am sitting quietly looking around me. God wants me to be peaceful. I see everything that is wrong. I have noticed that when people try to hide their emotions they get pale. My mother-in-law and my wife were pale and trembled a little. I was not. It must be very difficult to hide emotions.

My wife came to me and told me to tell Kyra that I would not come back any more. My wife's eyes were full of tears and she said, trembling, that she would not leave me. I cried because God did not wish us to separate. I told her that.

I would not remain in Zurich if my wife is not frightened of me; but if she is afraid I would rather be in an asylum, as I fear nothing. Her soul was weeping. I felt my heart ache and said again that if she is not afraid of me I will come home again. She started crying and kissed me, saying that she and Kyra would never leave me whatever happens to me. I said, "Very well." She understood me and went away.

I want my manuscript to be photographed because I feel it is alive. I will give life to people by my manuscript if it is photographed. I see what a man is like by his face, and know that a man does not feel anxious if he has nothing to blame himself for. I will live in big hotels because I want everybody to see me. I want to stay in a simple hotel if my wife will let me. My wife says that she cannot live in a dirty hotel so I will have to have recourse to cunning so as not to go to a big hotel. I prefer to live in a flat. I will conquer everybody. I am not afraid of anything except spiritual death. I will not lose my reason but I will weep and weep. I will show my faults and my perfection, for I do not want people to be afraid of me. I am a loving man and people who are loving are simple people.

No artist can deceive God. I know what God is and I know what an artist is and therefore I am not afraid for myself. Clemenceau will suffer, but I hope he will see through the whole company of diplomats and will be able to protect France. I love France and wish her well. I can see through the whole clique which has started the war. Clemenceau is a rich man and is not in need of anything, and so I feel that he has not been "bought." The Lloyd Georgians buy people, not only with money but with promises. Clemenceau thought that it would be good for France to get Alsace-Lorraine; this question can only be settled peacefully. Clemenceau understood Wilson and has consented to his plan. The French like the Alsatians and many families are weeping; they feel that it is unjust that they should not belong to French territory. The French do not like the Germans—I

know how one can develop dislike for German people and I know who taught France to say *Boche*. I do
not want war, but would like everyone to live in
peace. One must not quarrel! One must not quarrel!
German children are crying for their fathers too. I
love the Germans, although I am not a German. I
am a man. I do not belong to any party. I understand the love of mankind. I want people to love
each other. I do not want horrors. I want paradise
on earth. I am God in man. Everybody will be like
God if they do as I say. I am a man with faults and I
want people to correct their faults. I do not like people who do not correct their faults. I am a man who
is trying to improve himself. I do not think of past
mistakes. I love animals but not ferocious ones! One
must not kill beasts because God has given them life.
Many say that man has been born out of his father's
seed and his mother's womb—but I say that the seed
does not come from the firstborn man but from God.
Some claim that man descends from the ape but the
ape has been created from God's seed too. Many will
say that the species of apes have evolved from something else—my reply to them is that this "something
else" is God. I am infinity. I am mind and mind is
infinite. I will never die but man's intelligence dies
with his body, as it is limited. People say that intelligence has created everything; the aeroplanes, Zep-

pelins. Aeroplanes and Zeppelins are created by intelligence because they have life in them. There is movement in an aeroplane, there is movement in a Zeppelin. The aeroplane was invented by a Frenchman. The French people feel God, but they do not yet understand Him and therefore make mistakes. The Zeppelin also is created by intelligence because it was invented on the same principle as an aeroplane; the idea of an aeroplane has been copied from a bird, but a bird is a living thing, while aeroplanes are made of aluminum. Scientists admire the Zeppelin, as they understand its value. A Zeppelin can carry a great number of people, and this is of great value in wartime. The Germans have many Zeppelins. They thought they would achieve a great deal with them, but it ended in a mass of dead people.

My wife's mother came into my room and excused herself. I wanted her to understand that it was quite unnecessary to ask to be excused, that people could come to see me without asking. I am not disturbed by noise and shouting, but can work in spite of it. She thought for a while and said that she realized that I was used to it and that it was a good thing. But as she said, "It was very good," she thought of something else—she must have misunderstood me. . . .

Death

My wife came in and kissed me—I thought that it was God and understood that there is God in love. I heard the voice of my little Kyra. She loves me; she started to cry when I told her that I was going away forever. She understood me and started to weep.

I want to show Louise this book in German so that she may read what I write about her. She is from Zurich and her name is Louise Hamberg. One day somebody will show her the parts in this book where I write about her. I love Louise and she loves me; I never flirted with her and so she grew even fonder of me. She never said anything to me about it, but I understood her. I felt that she loved me. . . .

I am writing in small handwriting because paper is expensive—this is the trick of the shops. They take advantage of the war. They are afraid that it will end soon. The shops say that the war has forced them to increase their prices. I have been to a shop. I walked into it because God ordered me to do so. I had no money. I asked for some school exercise books. There was a woman there who, I realized, must have a financial interest in the business, because she told me one price while the other saleswoman there told me quite a different one. The woman gave me a very high price, the other a much smaller one. I followed the woman, and the other one became nervous.

I knew these kinds of shops—I used to buy the paints and papers for my *décors* at them. I did not mind spending money. The paints and paper were very expensive. Seeing how costly it was, I nearly gave up my work, but God said He would help me. I believed Him and continued buying lots of paper and paint. Paint can get dry but I know how to dilute it. The shops charge a lot for everything they sell, saying that the war is to be blamed for the high prices. I knew all the tricks of the shop, because I lived a long time in the Engadine, over a year. God was with me—I worked every day. I slept and thought of God. People say that a man cannot sleep and think at the same time. They are right: I do not think when I sleep—I feel. Understand that I do not think when I write—*I feel*.

Many shopkeepers deceive people. I will no longer write in large handwriting—I will write in small letters and save paper. The shopkeepers think that people who have money are stupid. It is not the people who are stupid, but the shops, because they sell in order to get money and not to serve people. I love mankind and do not deceive people.

I know what starts wars—they are started by commerce; this is a dreadful thing. It is the death of mankind. If people do not change their mode of life, commerce will destroy everybody. Commerce is an empty thing. People who are engaged in commerce seldom feel God—and God does not love them. God likes people who work. I want everybody to love, and to live. I like things I need, but do not want things I do not need. When I like a thing, I look after it. I bought three exercise books and paid a high price for them; one of the women deceived me. I do not like shops. I would like all factories to be destroyed because they spoil the earth. I love the earth and want to protect it.

I do not want pogroms. I want mankind to realize that one must give up all bad things because we do not live long. The earth is suffocating. Everybody hates earthquakes and asks God to save them from such calamities. I want earthquakes, because I know that then the earth can breathe. People do not know what earthquakes are and blame God. People will tell me that I am mistaken because I have not studied and know nothing about the earth, but I know I feel the earth. I do not think about it. The earth is alive. It was once a sun. The stars which twinkle are small suns, but the moon, and other planets like Mars, are not. There are no people on Mars. People will get frightened of me because I speak of things I have never seen, but I can see without using my eyes. I am feeling. Blind people will understand me if I tell them that eyes are no longer needed. People on some planets live in peace and love. All the astronomers will shout at me and say that Nijinsky is an ignorant stupid, and does not know a thing about astronomy. The astronomers have invented telescopes to study the atmosphere. People will say that I am insane because I speak of things I do not understand. I do understand. I am the spirit in a man whose body is Nijinsky. I have eyes, but I know that if my eyes were gouged out, I would be able to live without them.

I know a blind French general who goes for a walk with his wife every day. He feels life. He thinks he is unhappy and to hide this smiles at everybody. I noticed him because he has a peculiar walk, and holds his head up. I realized that he was unhappy and pitied him. I liked him and wanted to tell him that I was not afraid of being blind but saw that he would not understand me, so decided to tell him later.

I know that Mars in uninhabited because it is a frozen body. Mars was like the earth, but that was many billions of years ago. The earth will also be like Mars but in a few hundred years hence. The earth is suffocating, therefore I am asking everybody to abandon factories and listen to me. I know that this is necessary for the salvation of the earth.

My caretaker is stupid—he drinks, imagining that

he is well, but he is killing himself. I am the Saviour. I am Nijinsky and not Christ. I love Christ, because He was like me. I love Tolstoy, because he was like me. I want to save the entire earth from suffocation. All the scientists must leave their books and come to me, and I will help everyone because I know so much. I am a man in God. I am not afraid of death. I beg people not to be afraid of me. I am a man with faults, like other people. I want to improve myself. I must not be killed because I love everyone equally.

I will go to Zurich and will see the town, which is a commercial town, and God will be with me.

I am not intelligence, but mind. Tolstoy spoke about the mind, Schopenhauer also. I too write about mind. My philosophy is truth and not invention. Nietzsche became insane because he realized at the end of his life that everything he had written was absurd. He became frightened of people and went mad. I will not be frightened if people throw themselves at me. I understand crowds. I can manage them, although I am not a commander. I like family life; I love all children, and I like to play with them. I understand them. I am a child, and I am a father. I am a married man. I love my wife and want to help her in life. I know why men run after girls. I know what a girl is. Man and woman are one; I prefer married people because they know life. Married people make mistakes but they live. *I am husband and wife in one.* I love my wife. I love my husband. I do not like a husband and wife to be debauched. I am a physical body but not physical love. I am love for mankind. I want the government to allow me to live where I like. My wife is a good woman, so is my child, and they shall not be hurt.

I will write a great deal because I want to explain to people the meaning of death and life. I cannot write quickly because my muscles are getting tired. I cannot any more. I am a martyr—I feel pain. I am fond of writing; I want to help people, but I cannot write because I am tired. I want to finish, but God does not let me. I write until God stops me.

PART THREE

THREE

FEELINGS

THE MAID was serving lunch to my wife, Kyra, and
the Red Cross nurse. Christ carried a large cross; the
nurse wears a small cross on a ribbon. Kyra wanted
to have a sweet. I told the nurse that the sweet would
be served when she had finished what was on her
plate. The little one was not hurt because she knows
that I love her, but the nurse felt differently, thinking that I wanted to correct her. The child is put to
bed after lunch; they think she is a weak creature,
but she is very strong. I cannot write, my wife disturbs me. She is thinking the whole time about costumes. I do not bother about them. She is afraid I
will not be ready.*

I do not want to dance after a meal, and therefore
will not start yet. I want to dance when I feel like it,
not when people are waiting for me, but I dislike to
keep people waiting, so will get dressed. I do not
want to quarrel and therefore will do everything I

---

*Referring to Nijinsky's last dance recital, which he gave by invita-
tion at the Suvretta House, St. Moritz, January, 1919.*

am told to do. I will go now to my dressing room—I have a lot of expensive clothes and will put on my best things so that everyone will think that I am rich. I will not make people wait for me, so will go at once.

I was upstairs a long time, slept a little; when I awoke I dressed and then went to the dressmaker. She had done her work very well. She understood me. She likes me because I give her presents. I wanted to help her but she does not like doctors. I told her to go to a doctor—she did not want to. I did not mind spending the money for it. I gave her husband a pair of knickers and she gave him this present, accepting it gratefully. She understood me, she did not feel offended. I like Negri—that is her name. She is a good woman. She lives very wretchedly—when I walked in I switched off the electric light in her house, which was not needed. She was not offended. I told her that she had done her work very well and that I will give her money and a present. She has no warm clothes so I will give her a warm sweater and cape to wear for going out. Although I dislike presents I like to give poor people what they need. She is cold and hungry but she is not afraid of work and therefore she has some savings. Her boy is six and her girl about two years old. I want to give a present to the

children too; they are very poorly dressed. I will give
her my sweaters and something else for the children.
I love children and they love me. She knows that I
love children. She feels that I am not pretending.
She knows I am an artist and she understands me.
She likes me and I like her. Her husband is a violin-
ist at the Palace Hotel, where people amuse themselves with all sorts of trifles. He is poor, he plays at
night. He is cold because he has no warm clothes. He
is fond of playing the violin and wants to study, but
he does not know how to do it as he has no time. I
want to help him but I am afraid he will not understand me.

I want to live a long time, my wife loves me very
much. She is afraid for me today—I acted very nervously. I behaved this way on purpose because the
public understands me better when I am vibrating.
They do not understand artists who are placid. One
has to be nervous. I offended the pianist Gelbar.* I
wish her well, but I was nervous. God wanted the
public to be in a state of excitement. The public came
to be amused and thought I danced for their amuse-
ment. My dances were frightening. They were afraid
of me, thinking I wanted to kill them. I did not. I
loved everybody but nobody loved me and I became

*Mme Gelbar, celebrated Viennese virtuoso, accompanied Nijinsky
this time.

nervous and excited; the audience caught my mood. They did not like me, they wanted to go away. Then I started to do a joyful, merry dance, and they began to enjoy themselves. First they thought I was a dull actor but I showed them that I could do merry things. The audience began to laugh when I did. I was laughing in my dance. The audience laughed—they had understood my dance and felt like dancing too.

I danced badly; I fell when I should not have. The audience did not care because my dancing was beautiful. They felt my mood and enjoyed themselves. I wanted to go on dancing but God said to me: "Enough." I stopped. The audience began to leave. The aristocrats and the rich people begged me to dance once more. I said that I was tired. They did not understand me, they insisted. I said to one of the aristocratic ladies present that her movements were exciting. She thought that I wanted to offend her. Then I explained that I meant that she had a feeling for movement; she thanked me for the compliment. I gave her my hand and she felt that I was right. I like her but I feel that she has come in order to make my acquaintance. She seems to like young men. I do not like this kind of life and therefore asked her to leave me. She guessed my feeling and did not continue the conversation. I wanted to talk to her but she did not feel like it. I showed her the blood on my foot—she does not like blood. I made her realize that blood is war and that I do not like war, and made her think about the riddle of life by showing her the dance of a cocotte. She did not go away because she knew that I was acting. The other people thought that I was going to lie down on the floor and would make love. Not wanting to embarrass the party, I got up when it was necessary. I felt the presence of God the whole evening. He loved me. I loved Him. "We were married." In the carriage when we were driving to the Suvretta I told my wife that today was the day of my "marriage with God." During the drive she understood me well, but at the party she lost "*this feeling.*" I loved her and therefore gave her some drink, saying I was well and happy. She felt differently then. She thought that I did not love her because I was nervous.

The telephone is ringing, but I will not answer it because I do not like to speak on the telephone. My wife wants to answer it. I walked out of the room and saw my wife in pyjamas; she likes to sleep in them. She loves me and therefore told me that it was time to go to bed. I went up and went to bed but I took my notebook with me to write down everything I have lived through today.

I lived through a great deal. Everything today was horrible. I am afraid of people—they neither feel nor understand me, they want me to live as they live. They want me to dance a merry dance. I do not like merriment, I like life. My wife is lying near me while I am writing. She is not asleep—her eyes are open. I stroked her gently. She has feeling and sensitiveness. I write badly as it is difficult. My wife is sighing— she feels me, I understand her and do not reply to her sigh. Today she loves me with feeling and in the spirit. Some day I will tell her that we must marry in spirit because I want spiritual love. I will tell her later, now she is afraid of me.

I cannot write; I have thought of a man who was at the party this evening.

My wife disturbs me, she feels everything. I laughed nervously. My wife is listening to the ringing of the telephone but she is thinking of me and my writing. She asked me what I was writing so quickly, and I closed my notebook because she wants to read it. She feels that I am writing about her but does not understand it, and is afraid for me. I want to write a lot today because I have much to say, but I want my wife to fall asleep. I know that I made a deep impression on her. She understood my feelings. She knows that I can act because she says that I act as well as Duse and Sarah Bernhardt. I have given her a great problem to solve. She cannot understand the meaning of death. She does not think of it as she does not want to die. She is yawning and thinks that I ought to sleep too. She is afraid also that I write nasty things about people. My wife is coughing and yawning to attract my attention.

I want artists to understand me and therefore I will share their life. If God wishes it I will go to a cabaret with them. There they lose all their feelings. They need money and I will give them some. They will forget me, but their feeling and sensitiveness will already be aroused. I want them to feel, therefore for several months I will dance in Paris to help the poor artists. If they want to organize the performance themselves, they can.

If they want me to organize it I will do so. But the expenses of my wife in Paris must be paid for. I will ask Astruc to call the poor actors and artists together because I want to speak to them. I will tell them: "Listen, I am an artist—and so are you. We are artists and therefore ought to love each other. Listen! I want to speak in a friendly way to you. Do you want me to?" I will ask them a question about life. If they understand me—I will be saved; if they do not feel and understand me—I will be a poor miserable man, and I will suffer. I do not want to dance in St. Moritz because people do not love me here. They think that I am ill. I am sorry. I am well but I do not save my strength. I will dance more than ever. I want to teach dancing and I will work a little every day. I will write also and won't go to any parties. I had enough of this sort of fuss. I do not like to be merry, because I know that merriment is death, the death of mind. I am afraid of death and therefore I love life.

I want to ask people to come and see me but my wife is afraid. I want to invite an old Jew who is a relation of Baron Gunsbourg. Baron Gunsbourg is a good man.

Everybody will say that Nijinsky has become insane. I do not care, I have already behaved like a madman at home. Everybody will think so, but I will not be put in an asylum, because I dance very well and give money to all those who ask me. People like an odd and peculiar man and they will leave me alone, calling me a "mad clown." I like insane people, I know how to talk to them. My brother was in the lunatic asylum.

I was fond of him and he understood me. His friends there liked me too. I was then eighteen years old. I know the life of lunatics and understand the psychology of an insane man. I never contradict them, therefore madmen like me. My brother died in an asylum.*

My mother is living through the last hours of her

* *Nijinsky's brother Stanislav died during the revolution when the asylums were opened and the inmates let loose.*

life. I am afraid I shall never see her again. I ask God to give her many more years to live! My mother and sister escaped from Moscow to get away from the Maximalists. They were tired of the Civil War, and escaped together with Kotchetovsky, my brother-in-law, and their daughter Ira, leaving all their belongings behind. They are good people. I am fond of my sister Bronia.* Kotchetovsky is a good man. He has a difficult life because he has to think about money. He loves painting and writing. He writes well.

The bell is ringing. It is A. returning from a party. She does not love me; she is fond of enjoying herself. A. wants me to take her into my company of dancers, but I cannot, as she has no feeling for work. She only wants to join my company as this would be convenient. She does not think of me; she does not care what I am doing. She amuses herself while I work and ignores my affection. I gave her a ring and clothes, I pretended to be in love with her, but she did not understand me. She drinks. My caretaker is a drunkard. He drinks without stopping, and he became ill. I told him long before that this would happen. He became ill and could not work and let the furnace go out—he let us freeze. It was during the time when I had to prepare my costumes with Negri.

---

*Nijinsky has one sister called Bronia (Bronislava Nijinska).

[167]

My wife does not shake when she dances. She is a healthy woman; her trouble is that she thinks too much. I am afraid for her, her thoughts will make it difficult for her to understand me. I am afraid, as she cannot follow my aims. She feels a great deal but she does not know the meaning of it. I am afraid to explain it to her because I know she will be frightened. I must improve her in a different way. She obeys me. I obey her. She will understand when other people will tell her that everything I do is all right.

I am in front of a precipice over which I might fall, but I am not afraid. God does not want me to fall. He helps me.

Once I went for a walk and it seemed to me that I saw some blood on the snow. I followed the traces of the blood and sensed that somebody *who was still alive* had been killed. I went in another direction and more traces of blood were visible. I was afraid but I followed the tracks; there was a precipice. I realized that the traces were not of blood but manure. Walking in the snow, I noticed the marks of skis which had apparently stopped near the traces of blood. I thought that someone had buried a man in the snow, having knocked him down and killed him. I got frightened and ran back. Later I returned again and felt that God wanted to see whether I was afraid of Him or not. I said aloud: "No, I am not afraid of God:

He is life and not death." Then God made me walk towards the precipice, telling me that He had been hurt and should be saved. I was afraid. I thought that the devil was tempting me, the same way as he did Christ. He was saying: "Jump down, then I will believe you." I was afraid and stood there for a little, then I felt that I was being drawn towards the precipice. I approached its edge and slipped, but some branches I had not noticed before stopped my fall. I was amazed and thought it was a miracle. God had wanted to try me. I understood Him. I tried to push the branches away but He did not allow me. For a long time I held on to them, then became terrified. God told me that I would fall if I let the branches go. Finally I disentangled myself from the bushes but did not fall. God said to me: *"Go home and tell your wife that you are insane."* I realized that God wanted to help me, and went home to bring this news to my wife.

On the way back again I saw the traces of blood, but no longer believed in their existence. God had shown me these in order that I should feel Him. I felt His presence and returned. He told me to lie down in the snow. I did so. He made me lie there for a long, long time. My hands began to get cold, to freeze. I took my hand off the snow and said that this could not be God's wish, as my hand was hurt-

[169]

ing. God was pleased, but after I had taken a few steps He ordered me to go back and lie down near a tree. I got hold of the tree, then slipped. God again commanded me to lie in the snow. I was lying there for a long time. I did not feel the cold any more— then God made me get up. I got up. He told me to go home. I went home. God said to me: "*Stop!*" I stopped. I again saw the traces of blood. He told me to return, I did. He said: "*Stop.*" I stopped.

Everybody will think that all this is my imagination, but I must say that everything I write is the absolute truth. I have lived through it. Everything I describe has happened to me. Somebody is knocking. Everyone in the house is asleep. Somebody outside the house called "*Oiga*" and keeps on shouting "*Oiga!*" Not wanting to wake my wife up, I do not want to move. My wife sleeps very well. I hope the servants will hear it and open the door. My notebook keeps on sliding; it is so uncomfortable. Somebody is walking up the stairs. I am not afraid. I believe it is A. returning from her party, but I am not sure. God knows, I do not. I am still only a man and not God. If God wishes it I will find out. God had made me understand that it was A. She sleeps in the next room, Kyra's bedroom is next to hers. Kyra sleeps soundly, therefore she could not have made the noise. The door was squeaking. I felt that it was A. I know how she moves, always nervously. She came home at a quarter past one at night. I looked at my watch which always goes correctly.

After having seen the traces I turned back, running quickly. I felt sure that someone had been killed. I realize also that someone must have tried to hide the marks of blood by covering them with snow so that it should look like manure. I looked closely and saw that it was dirt. After that I went back. The distance I had run was only about 10 meters—perhaps a little more. I ran very well. When I run I feel like a little boy. I ran home, pleased that my trials had ended, but God made me look at a man who was walking in my direction. God told me to go back, saying that "it was this man who had killed." I ran back. I stopped and hid myself behind a small hill, crouching so that the man could not see me, pretending that I had fallen in the snow and could not get up. I lay like this for a long time. Then I got up and turned round. I saw the man who shoveled the snow with a stick. Then he began to break some branches of a tree. I realized that he was looking for something. I was walking on the road on which the man was standing. He saw me but did not say anything—I wanted to greet him: "Good morning, old man," but he was too busy. I was not sure of what he was doing. After some time God told me to look back. I

[171]

did and saw the man digging again in the snow, with a stick, and I thought the stick would break. I felt that this man was the murderer. I knew I was wrong and in spite of this still felt that he was the murderer. I realized my mistake. I wanted to go but suddenly noticed a bench; near it was a heap of snow; in this mound of snow a piece of wood was stuck. The branch of a fir tree. It was broken in half. There was a big hole in the hillock of snow. I looked into it, thinking that this man must have put it there with a special purpose. It was a small mound and there was a cross on it—under the cross something had been written. I realized the man had arranged this grave, he thought of his wife. I was frightened and started to run, feeling that my wife had been taken ill. I am afraid of death and do not want it. I turned back and removed the bit of wood. Then I thought that the man. . . .

I ask the Swiss people to take care of me. I want to publish this book in Switzerland because I live here. I like Switzerland. I want to publish this book very cheaply. I want to make a little money because I am poor. I have no money, and do not like creditors, or to be in debt. I want to gamble on the Stock Exchange. With mind I will achieve more than with intelligence. I will produce a ballet in which I will portray mind and intelligence and the life of men—

but I must be helped in this task. I thought of Mr. Vanderbilt but have changed my mind. Vanderbilt lends money to artists. I do not like owing money to anybody and therefore I myself will earn the necessary amount to produce this new ballet. Diaghilev is a debtor. He thinks he has paid me back everything he owes, but he has lost the lawsuit in Buenos Aires. I won that lawsuit and have a judgment for 50,000 francs more. Diaghilev still owes me a great deal. I am not greedy but I want the money which I earned and which Diaghilev still owes me. I like money only because I can help with money.

Life is not sex—sex is not God. God is man, who fecundates only one woman, a man who gives children to one woman. I am twenty-nine years old. I love my wife spiritually, not for begetting children. I will have children if God wishes it. Kyra is an intelligent girl. I do not want her to be clever. I will prevent her from developing her intelligence. I like simple people but not stupidity, because I see no feeling in that. Intelligence stops people from developing. I feel God and God feels me.

I want to correct my faults but I do not know whether I will be able to. The doctor's eyes were full of tears when he told me that he needed no promises, he knew that I would do everything to stop my wife from being nervous and worried. I explained to

him that I was the one who wanted my wife's mother
to come, I do not want my wife to be afraid; therefore I wanted my mother-in-law to live with us. I am
not afraid of the Allied authorities. I do not care if
they take all our money.* But I do not want this
money to be taken on account of my family. I do not
want my wife to be ruined. I gave her all I had
which was very little, so that she should be able to
live. I am not afraid of life and therefore I do not
need money. My wife will weep if I die. I hope for
her sake that she will soon forget me. My wife does
not always understand or, rather, feel me. Tolstoy's
wife had no feeling. Tolstoy's wife cannot forget that
he had given all his money away. I want to give my
wife money. I love my wife and Kyra more than anybody else; my hand is tired.

I do not like Shakespeare's Hamlet because he reasons. I am a philosopher who does not reason—a
philosopher who feels. I do not like to write things
that are thought out. I like Shakespeare because he
loved the theater. Shakespeare understood the theater. I have understood the "living theater" also. I
am not artificial. I am life. The theater is not life. I
know the customs of the theater. The theater becomes

---

*Subjects of Allied countries were not allowed to spend money on the
subjects of the enemy countries. Mme Nijinsky's relatives were Hun-
garians.*

a habit. Life does not. I do not like the theater with a square stage. I like a round stage. I will build a theater which will have a round shape, like an eye. I like to look closely in the mirror and I see only one eye in my forehead. Often I make drawings of one eye. I dislike polemics and therefore people can say what they like about my book; I will be silent. I have come to the conclusion that it is better to be silent than to speak. Diaghilev told me to be silent. Diaghilev is clever. Vassilli, his servant, used to say, "Diaghilev hasn't got a penny, but his intelligence is worth a fortune." I say, "I haven't got a penny and no intelligence, but I have a mind." I call mind that center which generates feeling. I am sensitive. I was stupid before because I thought that happiness depended on money—now I no longer think it. Many people think about money, I need some to carry out my plans; we all have our plans and aims, and we earn money to realize them, but our problems are different. I am God's problem, not Antichrist's. I am not Antichrist. I am Christ. I will help mankind.

I will go to Geneva to have a rest because the doctor tells me to do so. He thinks I am tired because my wife is now very nervous, high-strung. I am not, therefore I will stay at home. My wife can go alone. She has a little money. I have not got a penny. I am not bragging when I say that I have no money. I like to have money and will earn some to give to my wife and to poor people. Many will say that Nijinsky pretends to be like Christ. I do not pretend—I love His deeds. I am not afraid of being attacked. I say everything I have to.

I used to go out on the street. I deceived my wife, I had so much semen that I had to throw it away. I did not waste it on a cocotte. I threw it on the bed in order to protect myself from catching a venereal disease. I am not erotic and therefore will not deceive my wife any more. My seed I will save for another child—I hope I will some day have a son. I love my wife, I do not want anything bad to happen to her. She is sensitive. She thinks that I do everything on purpose, in order to frighten her. Everything I do is for the purpose of making her well and happy. She eats meat—that causes her nervousness; it does not matter if one eats meat—to lead a good life is important. My wife knows that it is good to lead a regular life, but she does not realize what this mode of life consists of. "*To listen to God—and obey Him—that is a good regular mode of life.*" People do not understand God, and ask themselves who is this God who must be obeyed. I know God and His wishes. I love God.

I do not know what to write about, because I have suddenly thought of the doctors and my wife—who are talking in the next room. I know they do not like my actions but I will continue in the same way while God wishes it. I am not afraid of any complications. I will ask everybody to help me and will not be afraid if I am told this, for instance: "Your wife became insane because you have tortured her; for this you will be imprisoned for the rest of your life." I am not afraid of prison and there I will find life, but I will die there if I am put there for life. I do not wish my wife ill, I love her too much to harm her. I like to hide from people; I am used to living alone.

Maupassant was terrified of being lonely. The Count of Monte Cristo liked loneliness because he wanted time to prepare for his revenge. Maupassant was frightened of solitude; he loved people. I am afraid of loneliness but will not cry; God loves me and so I am not alone. If God leaves me I will die. As I do not want to, I will live like other people, in order to be understood by others. God is mankind, and does not like those who interfere with His plans. I do not; on the contrary I help Him. I am the weapon of God, a man of God. I like God's people. I am not a beggar. I will take money if a rich man will leave it to me. I like a rich man. The rich man has a lot of money and I have none. When everyone finds out that I have no money, they will get frightened and turn away from me. That is why I want to get richer every hour.

I will hire a horse and will make him take me home

without paying for it. My wife will pay. If she does not pay I will find a way of paying myself. I want my wife to love me and so I do all this to develop her character. Her intelligence is well developed but her feelings are not. I want to destroy her intelligence; then she can only develop in other ways. People think that without intelligence a man is either insane or a fool. An insane person is a person who cannot reason. A lunatic does not realize what he is doing. I understand my good and my bad actions. I am a man who has reason. In Tolstoy's book a lot is explained about reason. I read this book and therefore know what it means. I am not afraid of intelligent people. I am strong because I feel all that is said about me. I know that they invent all sorts of things to calm me. The doctors are good. My wife is also a good woman, but they think much too much. I am afraid for their intelligence. People went mad because they thought too much—I am afraid for them, they think too much. I do not want them to become insane: I will do everything to make them healthy.

I offended my wife without realizing it—then I asked her forgiveness; my faults were continuously being brought up at a suitable moment. I am afraid of my wife; she does not understand me. She believes that I am insane or wicked. I am not wicked, I love her. I write about life, not death. I am not Nijinsky as they think. I am God in man. My wife is a good woman. I told her in secret all my plans, then she told the doctors everything, believing this would help me. My wife does not understand my object; I did not explain it, not wanting her to know. I will feel and she will understand. She will feel and I will understand. I do not want to think, thinking is death. I know what I am doing. "*I do not wish you ill. I love you. I want to live and therefore I will be with you. I spoke to you. I do not want intelligent speech.*" The doctors speak with intelligence, so does my wife. I am afraid of them. I want them to understand my feelings. "*I know that it hurts you. Your wife is suffering because of you.*" I do not want death to come and therefore I use all kinds of tricks. I will not reveal my object. "*Let them think you are an egoist. Let them put you in prison. I will release you because you belong to me. I do not like the intelligent Romola. I want her to leave you. I want you to be mine. I do not want you to love her as a man loves. I want you to love her with a sensitive love. I know how to simplify and smooth everything that has happened. I want the doctors to understand your feelings. I want to scold you because the doctors think that your wife is a nervous woman. Your cross* has done so much harm that you cannot disentangle it all. I know your faults because I have committed them.*" I put on a cross

---

Nijinsky wore a cross over his necktie and walked around St. Moritz, causing a sensation, described in the biography.

on purpose: "*She understood you. The doctor came in order to find out what your intentions are and does not understand anything at all. He thinks and therefore it is difficult for him to understand. He feels Romola is right and that you are right too. I know how to understand.*" I think better than doctors. "*I am afraid for you, because you are frightened. I know your habits. Your love for me is infinite; you obey my orders. I will do everything to make you understand, I love your wife and you. I wish her well. I am God in you. I will be yours when you will understand me. I know what you are thinking about: that he is here and is staring at you. I want him to look at you.*" I do not want to turn round because I can feel him looking at me. "*I want to show him your writing. He will think that you are ill because you write so much. I understand your feelings. I understand you well. I am making you write with a purpose because he will understand your feelings too. I want you to write everything I am telling you. People will understand you because you are sensitive. Your wife will understand you also. I know more than you and therefore I ask you not to turn around. I know your intentions. I want to carry out our plans but you must suffer. Everybody will feel and understand only when they see your sufferings.*"

I want to write about my conversation in the dining room with my wife and the doctor. I pretended I was an egoist because I wanted to touch him. He will be offended if he finds this out but I do not care. I do not divide love. I wrote that I loved my wife better than anybody—I wanted to show how I feel about my wife. I love A. just as much. I know her tricks. She understands my feelings because she is going away in the next few days. I do not want her presence. I want my mother-in-law to come because I want to study her and help her. I do not study people's character in order to write about them. I want to write in order to explain to people their habits—which lead them to death. I call this book "Feelings." I love feeling and will write a big book about it. There will be a description of my life in it. I do not want to publish this book after my death. I want to publish it now. *"I am afraid for you because you are afraid for yourself. I want to say the truth. I do not want to hurt people. Perhaps you will be put in prison for writing this book. I will be with you because you love me. I cannot be silent. I must speak. I know you will not be put in prison; legally you have not committed an offense. If people want to judge you, you shall answer that everything you said is God's word. Then they will put you into an asylum, and you will understand insane people. I want you to be put in a prison or into an asylum. Dostoievsky went to the gallows and therefore you also can go and sit somewhere. I know people whose love is not dead and they will not allow you to be put anywhere. You will become as free as a bird when this book is published in many thousands of copies. I want to sign the name of Nijinsky—but my name is God. I love Nijinsky not as Narcissus but as God.*" I love him because he gave me life. I do not want to pay any compliments. I love him. He loves me because he knows my habits. "*Nijinsky has faults, but Nijinsky must be listened to because he speaks the words of God.*" I am Nijinsky. "*I do not want Nijinsky to be hurt and therefore I will protect him. I am only afraid for him because he is afraid for himself. I know his strength. He is a good man. I am a good God. I do not like Nijinsky when he is bad.*" I do not like God when he is bad. I am God, Nijinsky is God. "*He is a good man and not evil. People have not understood him and will not understand him if they think. If people listened to me for several weeks there would be great results. I hope that my teachings will be understood.*" All that I write is necessary to mankind. Romola is afraid of me, she feels I am a preacher. Romola does not want her husband to be a preacher, she wants a young, handsome husband. I am handsome, young. She does not understand my beauty, I have not got regular features. Regular features are not like God. God has sensitiveness in the face, a hunchback can be Godlike. I like hunchbacks and other freaks. I am myself a freak who has feeling and sensitiveness, and I can dance like a hunchback. I am an artist who likes all shapes and all beauty. Beauty is not relative. Beauty is God, He is in beauty and feeling. Beauty is in feeling too.

I love beauty. I feel it and understand it. Those people who think write nonsense about beauty. One cannot discuss it. One cannot criticize it. I am feeling beauty. I love beauty.

I do not want evil—I want love. People think that I am an evil man. I am not. I love everybody. I have written the truth. I have spoken the truth. I do not like untruthfulness and want goodness, not evil. I am love. People take me for a scarecrow because I put on a small cross which I liked. I wore it to show that I was Catholic. People thought I was insane. I was not. I wore the cross in order to be noticed by people. People like calm men. I am not. I love life. I want it. I do not like death. I want to love mankind. I want people to believe in me. I have said the truth about A., Diaghilev, and myself. I do not want war and murders. I want people to understand me. I told my wife that I would destroy the man who would touch my notebooks, but I will cry if I have to do it. I am not a murderer. I know that everyone dislikes me. They think I am ill. I am not. I am a man with intelligence.

The maid came and stood near me, thinking that I was sick. I am not. I am healthy. I am afraid for myself because I know God's wish. God wants my wife to leave me. I do not want it, I love her and will pray that she may remain with me. They are telephoning

[183]

about something. I believe they want to send me to prison. I am weeping, as I love life, but I am not afraid of prison. I will live there. I have explained everything to my wife. She is no longer afraid, but she still has a nasty feeling. I spoke harshly because I wanted to see tears—but not those which have been caused by grief. Therefore I will go and kiss her. I want to kiss her to show her my love. I love her, I want her, I want her love. A. has felt that I love her too and she is remaining with us. She is not leaving. She has telephoned to sell her ticket. I do not know for certain but I feel it.

My little girl is singing: "Ah, ah, ah, ah!" I do not understand its meaning, but I feel what she wants to say. She wants to say that everything—Ah! Ah!—is not horror but joy.

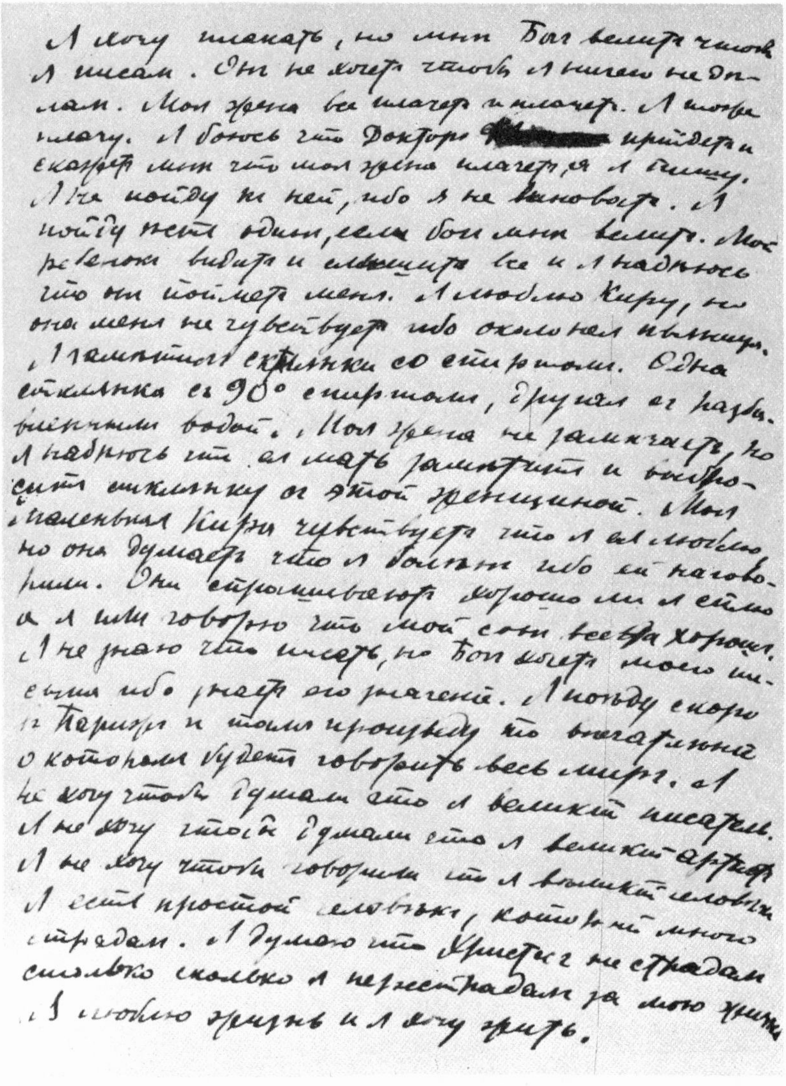

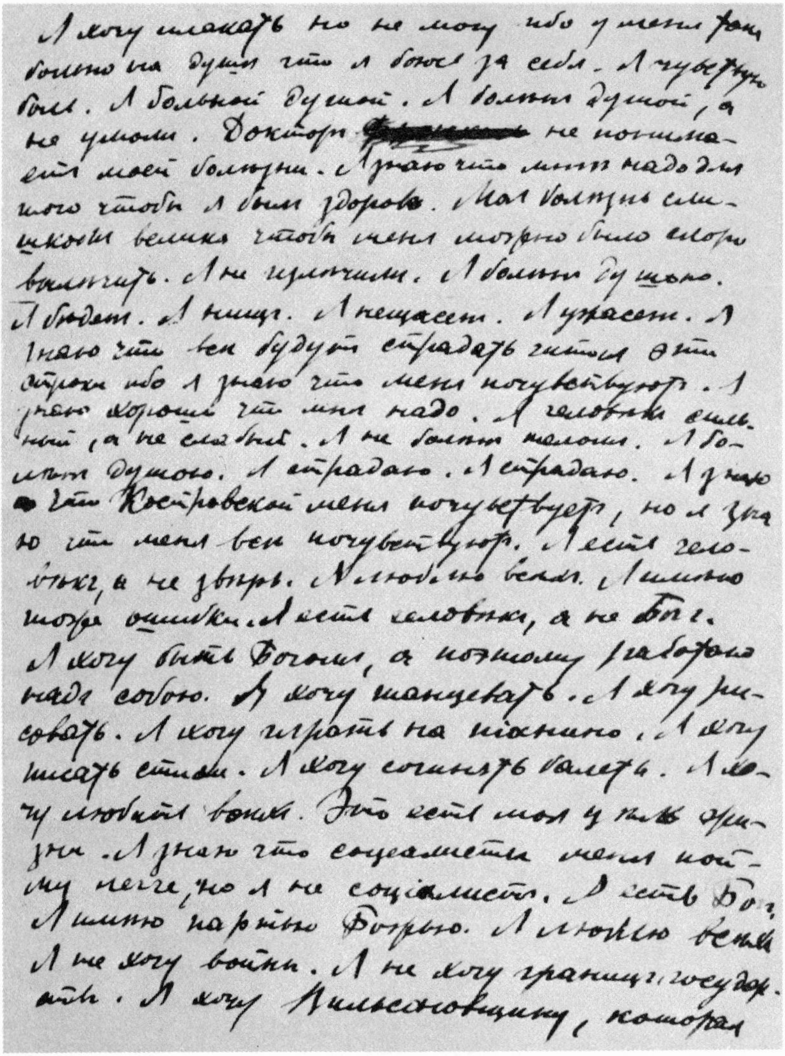
Я хочу плакать но не могу ибо у меня так
больно на душе что я боюсь за себя. Я чувствую
боль. Я больной душой. Я болен душой, а
не умом. Доктора не понима-
ют моей болезни. Я знаю что мне надо для
того чтобы я был здоров. Моя болезнь слиш-
ком велика чтобы меня можно было скоро
вылечить. Я не излечим. Я болен душою.
Я беден. Я нищ. Я несчастен. Я ужасен. Я
знаю что все будут страдать читая эти
строки ибо я знаю что меня почувствуют. Я
знаю хорошо что мне надо. Я человек силь-
ный, а не слабый. Я не болен телом. Я болен душою. Я страдаю. Я страдаю. Я знаю
что Костровский меня почувствует, но я зна-
ю что меня все почувствуют. Я есть человек, а не зверь. Я люблю всех. Я имею
тоже ошибки. Я есть человек, а не Бог.
Я хочу быть Богом, а поэтому я работаю
над собою. Я хочу танцевать. Я хочу ри-
совать. Я хочу играть на пианино. Я хочу
писать стихи. Я хочу сочинять балеты. Я хочу любить всех. Это есть моя цель жиз-
ни. Я знаю что социалисты меня пой-
мут лучше, но я не социалист. Я есть Бог.
Я имею партию Божью. Я люблю всех.
Я не хочу войны. Я не хочу границ государ-
ств. Я хочу Вильсоновщину, которая

Facsimile of Nijinsky's Epilogue

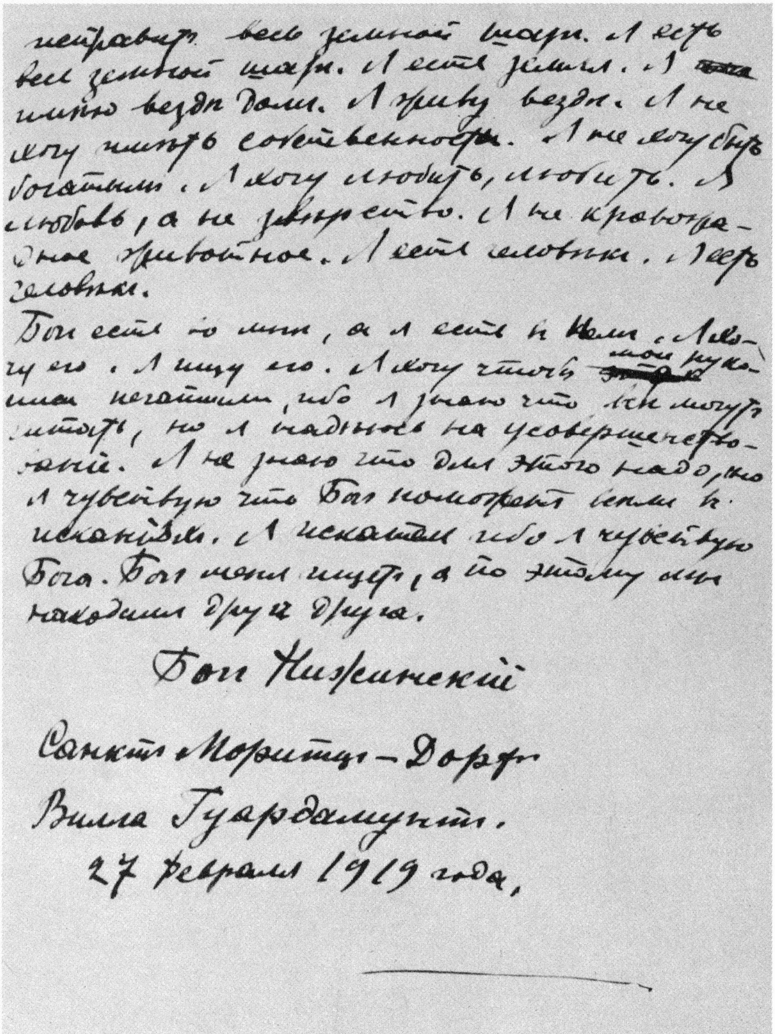

исправить весь земной шар. Я есть весь земной шар. Я есть земля. Я ~~…~~ имею везде дом. Я живу везде. Я не могу иметь собственности. Я не могу быть богатым. Я могу любить, любить. Я любовь, а не зверство. Я не кровожадное животное. Я есть человек. Я есть человек.

Бог есть во мне, а я есть в Нем. Я хочу его. Я ищу его. Я хочу чтобы мои рукописи печатались, ибо я знаю что все могут читать, но я надеюсь на усовершенствование. Я не знаю что для этого надо, но я чувствую что Бог поможет всем ищущим. Я искатель, ибо я чувствую Бога. Бог меня ищет, а поэтому мы находим друг друга.

Бог Нижинский

Санкт-Мориц-Дорф.

Вилла Гуардамунт.

27 февраля 1919 года.

Facsimile of end of Epilogue

Vaslav Nijinsky in 1913

EPILOGUE

I WANT TO CRY but God orders me to go on writing. He does not want me to be idle. My wife is crying, crying. I also. I am afraid that the doctor will come and tell me that my wife is crying while I write. I will not go to her, because I am not to blame. My child sees and hears everything and I hope that she will understand me. I love Kyra. My little Kyra feels my love for her, but she thinks too that I am ill, for they have told her so. She asks me whether I sleep well and I tell her that I always sleep well. I do not know what to write, but God wishes me to. Soon I will go to Paris and create a great impression—the whole world will be talking about it. I do not wish people to think that I am a great writer or that I am a great artist nor even that I am a great man. I am a simple man who has suffered a lot. I believe I suffered more than Christ. I love life and want to live, to cry but cannot—I feel such a pain in my soul—a pain which frightens me. My soul is ill. My soul, not my mind. The doctors do not understand my illness. I know what I need to get well. My illness is too great to be cured quickly. I am incurable. My soul is ill, I am poor, a pauper, miserable. Everyone who reads these lines will suffer—they will understand my feelings. I know what I need. I am strong, not weak. My body is not ill—it is my soul that is ill. I suffer, I suffer. Everyone will feel and understand. I am a man, not a beast. I love everyone, I have faults, I am a man—not God. I want to be God and therefore I try to improve myself. I want to dance, to draw, to play the piano, to write verses, I want to love everybody. That is the object of my life. I know that Socialists would understand me better—but I am not a Socialist. I am a part of God, my party is God's party. I love everybody. I *do not* want war or frontiers. The world exists. I have a home everywhere. I live everywhere. I do not want to have any property. I do not want to be rich. I want to love. I am love—not cruelty. I am not a bloodthirsty animal. I am man. I am man. God is in me. I am in God. I want Him, I seek Him. I want my manuscripts to be published so that everybody can read them. I hope to improve myself. I do not know how to, but I feel that God will help

all those who seek Him. I am a seeker, for I can feel
God. God seeks me and therefore we will find each
other.

GOD AND NIJINSKY,
Saint Moritz-Dorf,
Villa Guardamunt
February 27, 1919

Edited by ROMOLA NIJINSKY,
Easter, 1936
Sanatorium Bellevue,
Kreuzlingen